W9-BVA-859

MALAY PEASANT SOCIETY
IN JELEBU

LONDON SCHOOL OF ECONOMICS
MONOGRAPHS ON SOCIAL ANTHROPOLOGY

Managing Editor: Anthony Forge

The Monographs on Social Anthropology were established in 1940 and aim to publish results of modern anthropological research of primary interest to specialists.

The continuation of the series was made possible by a grant in aid from the Wenner-Gren Foundation for Anthropological Research, and more recently by a further grant from the Governors of the London School of Economics and Political Science. Income from sales is returned to a revolving fund to assist further publications.

The Monographs are under the direction of an Editorial Board associated with the Department of Anthropology of the London School of Economics and Political Science.

LONDON SCHOOL OF ECONOMICS
MONOGRAPHS ON SOCIAL ANTHROPOLOGY
No. 29

MALAY PEASANT SOCIETY IN JELEBU

BY

M. G. SWIFT

UNIVERSITY OF LONDON
THE ATHLONE PRESS
NEW YORK: HUMANITIES PRESS INC.
1965

First published by
THE ATHLONE PRESS
UNIVERSITY OF LONDON
at 2 Gower Street, London WC1
Distributed by Constable & Co Ltd
12 Orange Street, London WC2

Canada
Oxford University Press
Toronto

© *M. G. Swift,* 1965

Library of Congress Catalog Card No. 65–14844

Printed in Great Britain by
WESTERN PRINTING SERVICES LTD
BRISTOL

TO MY PARENTS

Preface

This book is a shortened version of a thesis presented for the Ph.D. degree in the University of London. Fieldwork was made possible by an award from The Treasury Committee for Studentships in Foreign Languages and Cultures, to whom go my sincere thanks.

I wish to acknowledge my great debt to Professor Raymond Firth for patient guidance and help, not only as supervisor of my graduate work, but throughout my training in anthropology.

My work in Malaya was made easier and pleasanter by the friendly helpfulness I met on all sides, whether amongst private individuals, or amongst all ranks, high and low, of Government service. I am especially grateful for the kindness of Enche Saidin bin Dain and of Mr. and Mrs. John Watts. To the people of Jelebu, especially my neighbours in the village where I lived, my debt is also great; here I would mention particularly Enche Hashim bin Bashir, Enche Mohd. Derus bin Yaakub, Almarhum Dato Panglima Perang Mahad and their families, and, above all, Enche Hussin bin Haji Abdul Rahman and his family.

To my many other friends who will know that they too deserve thanks and acknowledgement I can only plead the impossibility of mentioning everyone, and assure them that their kindness is gratefully remembered.

> *Hutang emas di-bayar emas,*
> *Hutang budi di-bawa mati.*

My thanks also go to my wife, both for help with the book itself, and above all for her continued patient encouragement.

Sydney, 1963   M.G.S.

Contents

MAP

TABLES

CHAPTER I
Introduction

This study of Malay peasant social organization in Jelebu is especially concerned with two topics, the matrilineal kinship system and the economy.

Jelebu is an administrative District of the Malayan State of Negri Sembilan, and was also a major district (*luak*) of the traditional polity. Negri Sembilan has attracted more anthropological attention than other parts of Malaya because of the matrilineal organization of the Malay inhabitants. They are organized into clans and subclans, which are grouped by districts under a chief (*undang*), selected from one of the clans, who rules with a council of the clan chiefs. All districts are united under the authority of a royal ruler (*Yang di Pertuan Besar* or *Yam Tuan*), who lives with other princes in the small central district of Sri Menanti. Royal title and office, unlike clan membership and office, are transmitted patrilineally.

In the past the main economic activity was the cultivation of rice in the narrow valleys of this hilly State, but in modern times the cultivation of cash crops, especially the growing of rubber on the hill slopes, has become of major importance. These modern economic changes have also favoured changes in the traditional arrangements concerning property and inheritance, which were formerly direct expressions of the kinship system. Traditional society has also been greatly affected by the growth, under British control, of modern administration.

Negri Sembilan provides a wealth of topics for anthropological research. The main features of the traditional society are only barely known, and many aspects of the dynamics of its operation await investigation. For example, the integration of Islam with its patrilineal emphasis into a strongly matrilineal society has often been mentioned as an interesting problem, but it remains one which has not yet been fully studied.

In the following discussion I shall be concerned with the

traditional organization only to the extent necessary to understand modern conditions. I started fieldwork with the hypothesis that modern economic changes had played a major part in inducing broader social change. More specifically I believed that the introduction of rubber had led to an individualization of the economy, and therefore to opposition to the traditional ownership of land by women as representatives of the matri-kin, and also to kinship restrictions on the rights of land-owners. Furthermore, I believed that these changes, starting from the economy, had spread into a general decline of the traditional kinship organization (Firth, 1951, pp. 107–8). Hence my special interest in the two topics mentioned above.

Apart from their interrelations the topics of matrilineal kinship and the economy are each interesting in their own right. The matrilineal organization of Negri Sembilan, and of the parent area of Minangkabau in Western Sumatra, have often been cited by students of kinship, but there is still no full published account of this system based on field research.[1] I want therefore to describe such aspects of this system as can still be studied in the field.

My analysis is also related to two growing fields of interest in contemporary social anthropology. One of these is the study of tribal and peasant economies called economic anthropology. The other is the discussion of peasantry which stems from the work of Redfield and recent studies of village society in Asia and Latin America. Both fields are joined in the peasant economy, and my description of Jelebu Malay economy, although largely confined to its relations with other aspects of village society, is also intended as a contribution to peasant studies.

CHARACTERISTICS OF THE DISTRICT OF JELEBU

Jelebu is the most isolated of the major areas of Negri Sembilan. Although only twenty-two miles from Seremban, the state capital, the road includes a tortuous eight-mile pass. It then winds slowly through the district before entering the sparsely populated Upper Pahang, or Kuala Pilah. Jungle paths connect Jelebu with the Ulu Langat area of Selangor, but this route is too difficult to have economic significance, and was, in any case, closed

---

[1] Professor P. E. De Josselin De Jong has written a valuable account of Negri Sembilan based on published sources (1951), and articles based on his fieldwork (1956 and 1960).

for security reasons throughout the Emergency (1948–1960).

Jelebu was also relatively isolated in the past when water transport was the principal means of communication in Malaya. The rivers of Jelebu drain towards Pahang and the east coast, unlike those of the rest of the state which flow to areas of greater population and development on the west coast.

In the early days of British control there was much tin mining in Jelebu, with its attendant disrupting consequences for Malay society, but deposits have long been exhausted near the main areas of Malay settlement. Similarly, the few large rubber estates are also distant from Malay settlement.

Surrounded by mountains, Jelebu is itself very hilly, with numerous small streams and rivers which gradually join the river Triang. Malay settlement follows the valley sides like a ribbon wherever the valley floor is level and wide enough to permit rice cultivation. Houses occupy the slopes immediately above the rice-fields. In some cases there may be several acres in one piece of homestead, with only one or two houses, but this land is never intensively cultivated, and is often not cultivated at all. The economic importance of homestead comes from fruit and coconut trees, from foraging for poultry, and, save in the few cases where it is fenced, from the grazing of goats. Behind the houses lie rubber smallholdings and orchards, giving way, as the land becomes more inaccessible, to jungle.

Villages are not nucleated. Houses form a narrow line following the valley contour, petering out as the valley narrows, and slightly thicker in places of longer settlement. A generation ago the picture would not have been so clear, for instead of a continuous ribbon there were only small strips in the most desirable positions. Population increase has been large, and this has led to a continuous increase in the land used for house sites.

In a few places the confluence of rivers and gentler terrain make possible a greater concentration of population. Even here the villages are not nucleated settlements, for the peasant likes to have some of each of the three categories of land, rice, rubber and homestead, within easy reach of his home, and has, moreover, a pronounced dislike of living too near his neighbours.

The report on the 1947 Census gives the population of Jelebu as 19,135, of whom 8,419 were Malays and 668 other Malaysians (Aborigines and Indonesians or people of Indonesian extraction who list themselves as such).[1] Also it may be seen that while there are differences in their concentration some Chinese are to be found in every *mukim*. Even where they were not allowed to own land under the Malay Reservation policy (International Bank 1955, p. 227), until the Emergency there were always some Chinese to be found living in close proximity to Malays.

One of the major means of fighting Communist terrorism was the policy of Resettlement, the concentration of the population so that they might be more easily controlled and protected, and prevented from aiding the terrorists. Resettlement on the whole affected the Chinese rather than the Malays, and this policy ended the intermingling of the populations. In the *mukim* where my work was concentrated there were no Chinese resident at all, save for a few individuals who had embraced Islam and 'become Malays'. Beginning in 1956 there was a gradual relaxation of rationing, curfews and the other Emergency Regulations, and Malay villagers who had been moved were allowed to return to their original villages. In August 1960 the Emergency was formally declared at an end and all the Regulations were repealed, but by December 1960 no Chinese had yet returned to live in the *mukim*.

This separation of the populations has had consequences for Malay society. With less frequent contact between the races personal friendships arising from daily contact, and some common economic activities, have been weakened or forgotten. This has reinforced the effect of the predominantly Chinese membership of the Malayan Communist Party, and the predominantly Malay membership of the Security Forces, in giving the Emergency the character of communal strife. Also the resettlement of the Chinese has hindered their economic activities in Malay villages as dealers and shopkeepers and has created opportunities for some Malays in these fields.

The town plays an important part in village life. It is the centre of administration, and the place where the villager disposes of his rubber and buys many of his consumer goods. As the Emergency Regulations allowed village shops to stock only a very limited range of goods, the Emergency has served to increase the importance of the town for the villagers.

The town is also a pleasantly bustling place of entertainment.

[1] The figures from the 1957 Census are: Population 23,325, Malaysians 12,570.

The cinema has an enthusiastic following. There is the certainty of meeting friends and relatives from neighbouring villages and being able to enjoy a long gossip, sitting in a coffee shop or standing about in groups in the streets. Even where people live nearer each other than they do to the town they may still rely on meeting there. Modern communications have also played a part in realigning village ties. A village that is quite near by jungle path may become distant when people give up using those paths and keep to roads where buses run, and bicycles can be ridden easily.

The research on which this study is based falls into two phases. From October 1954 until July 1955, and from April until December 1956, I was continuously engaged in field research. It is from this phase that the main body of my material derives.

In September 1957 I returned to Malaya, where I lived until December 1960. I was therefore able to return continually to the scene of my fieldwork, and also to obtain a comparative knowledge of some other parts of Malaya. On brief visits I had to rely more on reports from informants than I would normally feel acceptable, and I therefore treat material collected during this second phase as a supplement rather than part of the material gained as a participating observer. The political changes which have followed independence (August 1957) are particularly important. During visits I have been able to form impressions of how these changes have affected village society, but cannot presume to analyse them without further detailed study. As a consequence, the 'ethnographic present' of this account is the period immediately preceding the transfer of power.

Research was carried out with the usual participant observation methods, employing the vernacular. The suspicion arising from the Emergency was a serious complicating factor. Jelebu was then a 'very Black Area', to use the jargon of the time, and some of the villagers amongst whom I lived had been involved with a Communist food-collecting team, and the whole village was living under the threat of resettlement. As I was believed to be a Government agent investigating the villagers there were considerable restrictions on my ability to show too much curiosity about people's affairs. Bias may have arisen from my need to extend my inquiries from my friends to their kin and friends; by this means avoiding much of the suspicion, but perhaps not getting a random sample.

The curfew may also have made my material atypical. During my first visit the people were legally confined to their houses from 10 p.m. until 6 a.m., and during the second visit from 6.30 p.m. until 6 a.m. Such rules cannot be strictly enforced in a village, but they still seriously affected participation in collective events, altered their character and lessened their occurrence. This effect was particularly felt because of the strategic position of the District capital at the centre of Malay settlement. When the gates of the town were shut each night all traffic within the District stopped. I also feel that the effects of the curfew may have led me to underemphasize the role of religion in village life in normal times, for during the Emergency only people who lived very close to the mosque were free to go there of an evening and return when they wished. Even so, the end of the Emergency has not led to any marked increase in celebrations at night at either the mosque or the village prayer house.

All vernacular words frequently used may be found in the glossary. In the romanization of Malay words I have followed modern practice as exemplified in the newspaper *Berita Harian*. The most important single difference from pre-war usage is that the silent vowel ĕ is spelled e, and also, important here, *pĕsaka*, inheritance, is spelled *pusaka*. A good simple pronunciation rule is 'English consonants, continental vowels'.

Monetary values are expressed throughout in Malayan (Straits) Dollars. The Malayan dollar is worth 2s. 4d. or U.S. 33 c.

One of the most frequently used Malay words in this book is *adat*. This may loosely be translated as custom, but Wilkinson's Malay–English Dictionary gives as many as eleven ways in which the word may be used. Malay sources stemming from the Minangkabau tradition commonly distinguish four types of *adat*.

i. *Adat yang sa-benar-nya adat*. *Adat* which is really *adat*, the way of things as set out by God.

ii. *Adat istiadat*. The laws and arrangements made by Dato Perpateh nan Sabatang, the founding culture hero.

iii. *Adat nan di-adatkan*. Custom made after proper agreement and ceremony. This may be changed to meet changing conditions.

iv. *Adat nan teradat*. Mere conventional usage (Ahmad 1956. 110).

Although in Negri Sembilan *adat* may be used in any of its many meanings the most common and most important use is to refer to the traditional matrilineal organization in all its various aspects, kinship, legal, political, economic etc. The reference is therefore largely to meanings ii and iii, to a system of rules which are validated by tradition, and also to the offices and objects which express these rules. The *adat* is a valued possession of which the Malay is proudly conscious. It embodies his superiority to other groups, even though they may be richer and more powerful. I felt that to translate *adat* simply by the broad term custom would make for confusion, and have therefore left it untranslated when it refers to the explicit rules of the matrilineal system. I have also used it as an adjective when referring to things which pertain to that system, e.g. *adat* chief, *adat* office.

CHAPTER II

The Traditional Political System

This account of the traditional political system is partly a reconstruction, using literary sources and the memories of informants, as well as observation where the system is still operating It is no longer possible to draw a complete picture of the traditional polity from the traces still preserved.

A particularly important source of *adat* knowledge is a large body of sayings (*perbilangan adat*), a largely oral tradition which gives validity and continuity to kinship behaviour. In poetic form, and open to argument and interpretation, the sayings embody the code which governed behaviour between individuals and groups (Caldecott, 1917). Although there is some variation to suit local conditions these sayings are very much alike throughout Negri Sembilan, and are also similar to sayings of the same kind in Minangkabau.

Nowadays extensive knowledge of the sayings is the preserve of a few old men. But this may well have always been the case. The sayings speak of the elders as guiding the group, and expertise in *adat*, implying a willingness to spend long hours matching and weighing sayings, and years of accumulated wisdom, is regarded as especially appropriate to the role of old man.

Even so, the high prestige value of being 'learned in custom', and the ceremonial importance of the sayings, give all men an incentive and opportunity to learn at least some of them. 'Reading custom' is an integral part of most ceremonies. For example, at the presentation of the ring which constitutes betrothal, at least one senior male from each of the two groups to be allied by the marriage sit facing each other, and in a formal manner exchange speeches derived from the sayings. The onlookers carefully follow these exchanges, silently appreciating the efforts of their own representative and endeavouring to find fault with that of the other group. Some knowledge of the sayings is essential for anyone who wishes to play fully his part as a man, and knowledge beyond the minimum is a matter for pride and a qualification for *adat* office.

The sayings also have a place in everyday life. Capping quotations, or attempting to prove others wrong in their interpretation of sayings, is a common pastime in coffee shops or at social gatherings.

The traditional system of political and social relations called *adat* is more than a norm to which events tended to conform in the past. It is also invested with high moral value, so that right behaviour according to *adat* is often spoken of in the same terms as right religious conduct, and this view is embodied in the sayings.[1] To the outsider, including other Malays, and even to some members of the society, there would seem to be considerable contradiction between matrilineal custom and Islam, but this is minimized, or even denied by the villagers, while religious institutions are given a kinship character. *Wakaf*, property devoted to religious purposes, is regarded as clan property. Even succession to offices in the mosque, such as *imam*, *katib* and *bilal*, are regarded as the birthright (*pusaka*) of the kin-groups with clan lands around the mosque.

THE HISTORICAL SETTING

The Malay population of Negri Sembilan claim descent from immigrants from Minangkabau.

A common thread runs through all legends of the first settlers. They are said to have married aboriginal women, thus acquiring rights to land, while the aboriginal men returned to the hills, leaving the lowlands and their sisters to the Malays. Such myths were the charter for the immigrants' possession of land, their superior rights as against later immigrants, and their former relations with the aborigines, involving, for example aboriginal participation in the selection of Malay chiefs, and Malay confirmation of aboriginal chiefs. Nowadays this earlier relationship with the aborigines no longer exists, although older men remember it, and occasionally reflect it in their use of terms such as *waris* and *biduanda* (which imply an honoured position) for the aborigines rather than the commoner but rather derogatory *rayat*. The

---

[1] A relevant and well-known saying is 'Custom is framed (*bersendi*) by religious law, religious law by God's book. Custom does not complain if religion is strong, religion does not complain if custom is strong. Agreement is the mother (*ibu*) of law and custom.'

increasing cultural gap between the Malays and the remaining jungle-dwelling aborigines leads young Malays to deny the relationship that their *adat* tells them exists.

The emergence of Negri Sembilan as a political unit may be dated from 1773, when Raja Melewar, a prince of the Minangkabau ruling house at Pagar Ruyong, was invited to become ruler, and founded the dynasty which still occupies the throne.

Migrants from Minangkabau had been living in the area for centuries before this, at one time under the control of Malaka, then the fief of the Bendahara of Johore, and then one of the prizes in the fighting between Johore, the Bugis and the Dutch. The weakening of control from Johore provided an opportunity, and the threat of the Bugis and the Dutch an incentive, for the request for an overlord. But beliefs about the importance of a Raja for a properly ordered country, part of a widespread Indonesian tradition of kingship, probably also played an important part in this desire for a Ruler. The sayings place great emphasis on the role of the Raja, as also do the sayings in Minangkabau, although in both areas the Ruler was largely confined to a symbolic supremacy.

Islam supports rather than challenges this earlier tradition, for the Raja is regarded as Caliph, the representative of God in his realm. In Negri Sembilan even constituent parts of the state, such as Jelebu, wished to have a Raja to live amongst them, although they were not willing to be ruled.

Subsequent history is a confused tale of prolonged strife, with rival claimants to the overlordship, and competition between locally born princes and others coming from Sumatra to claim the title (Wilkinson, 1912). The notion of delegation from the Ruler of Minangkabau was important at least until the 1860's, though, in fact, from the accession of Raja Radin until the present day, the title has descended within the Negri Sembilan branch of the royal house. The Padri War in Sumatra, which saw the end of the Sultanate at Pagar Ruyong, and the related falling of Minangkabau into the hands of the Dutch, were important here.

The growing importance of tin in the nineteenth century added to the disorder. Tin revenues increased both the stakes in struggles for power and office, and the resources available for these struggles. Tin also attracted outside attention, and the eventual extension of British control imposed order. The end of this phase may be

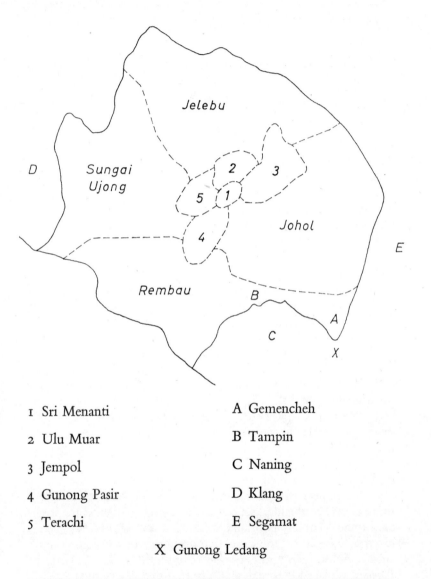

1 Sri Menanti

2 Ulu Muar

3 Jempol

4 Gunong Pasir

5 Terachi

A Gemencheh

B Tampin

C Naning

D Klang

E Segamat

X Gunong Ledang

TRADITIONAL POLITICAL BOUNDARIES IN NEGRI SEMBILAN

This map has been taken with kind permission from Professor De Jong's
Minangkabau and Negri Sembilan.

dated from the 1898 agreement which established the state in its present form.

The Position of the Ruler

The Yang-di-Pertuan-Besar (or Yam Tuan) of Negri Sembilan is the ruler of all the State, but historically the rights and duties implied by this rule varied considerably between the different constituent areas of the State. The situation may be conceived as two concentric circles around the small royal core of Sri Menanti (see map). In Sri Menanti the main authority belonged to the Tenku Besar, and other princes, under the Yam Tuan, with some other important offices the preserve of the Batu Hampar clan (also known as the *Ayer Kaki* or water of the feet). The special position of this clan was explained by a tradition making them the matrilineal kin of the Yam Tuan.

The next circle comprises four districts, Terachi, Gunong Pasir, Jempol and Ulu Muar, which, together with Sri Menanti, are known as 'enclosed lands'. The chiefs of these districts were not royal, but royal control and influence were still important, for example in such matters as choice of the local chiefs (A. Aziz, 1936, A. Kahar, 1960).

The outer circle is composed of the territories of the four chiefs (*luak undang nan empat*), the districts of Sungei Ujong, Jelebu, Johol and Rembau. Here the position of the Ruler was almost entirely nominal and symbolic, power lying with the *Undang* (district chief) and the clan chiefs.

The four *Undang* choose the Ruler from among the eligible group of princes. In the troubled times of the nineteenth century they continually engaged in king-making. For long periods different *Undang* supported rival claimants, and used the over-lordship as part of their own search for power.

In one respect British rule served to make conditions conform more closely to the ideal set out in the sayings. Whereas the Ruler used to be relatively poor and weak he was now formally recognized as exercising 'the executive authority of the state', and a large civil list, many times greater than the allowances paid to the *Undang*, replaced the small and uncertain income of the past.

But his new power is that of agent of the administration. 'Matters of Malay custom and religion' remained the province of the *Undang*, each in his district, and even modern reforms in this area require the concurrence of the four *Undang*. Informants stated that Dato Abdullah (*Undang* Jelebu 1905–1945) used to say that he was *raja* in Jelebu, and that if the Yam Tuan wished to be *raja* he had better stay in Sri Menanti. True or not, this illustrates well the prevailing view that the Ruler has no power in the internal affairs of the *luak*.

Under traditional arrangements the Ruler had certain specific powers and rights as well as his vague symbolic supremacy. For example, he alone was entitled to execute by beheading. He was *keadilan*, the fount of justice, although this can have meant little given his lack of practical power, while justice is exercised now by Courts organized on a Federal basis, falling under the authority of neither *Undang* nor *Raja*.

Again, the *Raja* is *berkhalifah*, God's viceroy. But in the past religion was either the concern of the kin groups, or in the hands of the *Undang*, who appointed the *Kadi* within his *luak*. Nowadays religious matters are increasingly coming under the control of the Government's Department of Religious Affairs, although this development often meets strong opposition in the villages. In the past Negri Sembilan did not possess a well-organized system of religious law, with courts and punishments for offences such as failing to observe the Fast, controlled by a Chief Kadi answerable to the Ruler.

The sumptuary rules and perquisites of the Ruler were important as symbols. Certain items of regalia, styles of housebuilding and decoration were his exclusive prerogatives. Some of these privileges have been formally surrendered, others have lapsed, while some are still observed, although for their observance they rely more on the Malay fear of shame (*malu*) and feelings of appropriateness than on organized sanctions.

The *Undang* and the *Luak*

For the rest of this chapter I shall be concerned with the internal organization of a *luak*, with particular reference to Jelebu.

Adat varies between the constituent parts of Negri Sembilan, and local experts speak of these variations as highly important. Structurally their main function is to serve as diacritical elements stressing the individuality of the various *luak* in the minds of their inhabitants. There are, for example, a few dollars difference between the marriage payments customary in each *luak*. Again, to symbolize his junior status, the *Undang* of Johol is supposed to wear his hair long.

Differences of this kind do not detract from the fundamental similarity of the matrilineal structure throughout the area, although one difference which sets Jelebu slightly apart from Rembau and Sungei Ujong should be mentioned. This is the absence of any dual division to parallel the *Baroh-Darat* (Lowland-Highland) division in Rembau (Parr and Mackray, 1910), and the *Ayer-Darat* (Water-Dryland) division in Sungei Ujong (Gullick, 1949).

The *Undang* of Jelebu is the ruler of the *luak*, subject only to the titular authority of the *Yam Tuan*. He is the holder of the powers attributed to the *Penghulu* in the *adat* sayings. But these powers are exercised with the concurrence of the eight chiefs (*lembaga*) of the matrilineal clans (*waris* or *suku*) who form the Council of Eight (*Orang Dilapan*). Their unanimous approval is necessary for his appointment, and if they are unanimous they can remove him from office.

The names of these eight clans, and the titles of their respective chiefs, are as follows:

Clan	Chief		
Waris Mentri	Dato Mentri Shahmang-kualam Rajasahari	*Waris Silasila*	*Biduanda*
Waris Ombi	Dato Ombi Pangkal Mahara-jalela		
Waris Kemin	Dato Maharaja Inda	*Waris Berundang*	
Waris Ulu Jelebu	Dato Raja Balang		
Waris Sarin	Dato Paduka Mentri		
Waris Tanah Datah	Dato Chinchang Maharaja Lela		
Waris Batu Belang	Dato Senara Angsa		
Waris Mungkal	Dato Mengiang Merah Bangsa		

Within this group of eight clans there are two divisions of major importance. The first five have superior status as *waris biduanda* or *waris negri*. This superiority is justified on the grounds of their prior settlement, while the other three clans were received by the *Biduanda*.

Apart from their right to superior office the status of the *Biduanda* is nowadays symbolized by the receipt of *hasil tanah*, compensation for *Biduanda* land rights which were commuted for money payment in 1891. These shares have become very small, perhaps as little as 20 c. a month, but the right to receive the sum is still jealously guarded.

Non-*biduanda* informants complained bitterly of the arrogance of the *Biduanda* in the past, up to, that is, the time of the Japanese Occupation, but the only concrete evidence of discrimination which I found was that previously only *Biduanda* were allowed to enter the Malay College at Kuala Kangsar (a school founded to train the children of princes and chiefs for Government service.)

The second important division is within the *Biduanda* itself. The Waris Mentri and the Waris Ombi are together known as the *waris silasila*, a name implying that they were the very first of all to arrive. Members of these two clans cannot occupy the position of *Undang*, but among the eight *lembaga* their chiefs occupy special and important positions.

The Dato Mentri is the tie of custom (*tali adat*). It is his right and duty to judge the suitability of all candidates for high office, including the *Undang*, according to the rules of *adat*. His long title calls him regent and prince for a day, for he is regent in periods when there is no *Undang*, and has the duty of supervising the selection, and carrying out the installation, of a new *Undang*. Should the clan qualified to provide a new *Undang* be unable to agree, or to find a candidate acceptable to the Council of Eight, the Dato Mentri has the duty of choosing the new *Undang* himself.

Informants especially interested in *adat* saw the Dato Mentri as exposed to supernatural danger because of the temptations of the *Undang*ship, to which he might approach so closely yet never achieve. They spoke of dangers such as death by madness, and, in the case of one famous Mentri who did try to become *Undang*, death by were-tiger (*Harimau keramat*).

In all matters the *Undang* should be approached through the Dato Mentri, who acts as a kind of vizier, although he, in turn, is required to make his approach through the chief of the *Undang*'s own clan, the 'bridge to the palace' (*titian ka-balai*).

The Dato Ombi is the lock of inheritance (*kunchi pusaka*), charged with the scrutiny of all candidates for office in terms of the inheritance rules.

Apart from their specific rights and duties the chiefs of the *waris silasila* have a general position of superiority *vis-à-vis* the other members of the Council of Eight, and have, in effect, a veto right with regard to all major offices within the *luak*.

The other three *biduanda* clans are known as the *waris berundang* because it is from them that the *Undang* is chosen. The right to select him passes in a fixed rotation from Ulu Jelebu to Sarin and then to Kemin. A saying has it that if the *Undang* is replaced after his death the office must rotate, but that if he is replaced while alive his successor may be drawn from the same clan. Expert opinion has it that the crucial point is whether he has been confirmed in office (i.e. has carried out the *tabal* ceremony). If the *Undang* dies before confirmation this is 'replace alive' (*ganti hidop*), and his clan may provide his successor, but if he be removed from office after confirmation, this would be 'replace dead' (*ganti mati*) and the office must rotate. This saying illustrates the ambiguity of the sayings as a constitution. I was discussing the point of succession at a time when it seemed likely that the *Undang* would be removed by unanimous agreement of the clan chiefs. Members of his clan insisted that since he was still alive the 'replace alive' rule must apply, while others preferred the interpretation given above.

As well as the major rotation between clans there is a less well-defined rotation among the constituent subclans of each.

The internal organization of a clan

Each clan is divided into a number of subclans (*perut*), each headed by a chief known as *ibubapa*. I translate *perut* as subclan rather than lineage because relationship within the group is largely putative, and not commonly traceable beyond two or three generations. The names of these subclans are usually also the names of villages which provide a territorial locus for the activities of the kin-group.

The *perut* is exogamous and marriage is matrilocal. Therefore a village must contain men who are not under the hereditary authority of the *ibubapa* of the village subclan, while its male members will be living in their wives' villages. A man maintains close ties with his own village, returning continually, often at intervals of days, and belonging there in a way he never can in his wife's village.

The sayings are quite explicit on the relationship between a man (*orang semanda*) and his wife's kin (*tempat semanda*). He is under their authority in every way, and has no right at all to intervene in the affairs of his wife's *perut*. In practice a man's interests and rights in his wife and children are recognized, but this is in spite of, rather than a part of, the matrilineal *adat*.

The *ibubapa* is chosen by election which must be unanimous. The principle of unanimity runs right through the traditional political and kinship structure of Negri Sembilan. In the *perut* failure to reach agreement means that the choice goes to the clan chief, even if he be of another subclan. Hence a majority candidate may have to be passed over for one to whom there are no strong objections. This rule may mean that the selection of a chief takes much time and discussion, and in some parts of the state has been replaced by majority voting, but it also lessens tensions and conflict which had to be avoided under traditional conditions where the total structure rested on the kinship organization.

Succession to the office of clan chief rotates among the constituent subclans. The order of rotation is in principle fixed, but is subject to adjustment, according to the availability of suitable candidates. This possibility of adjustment also allows heated differences to arise about which *perut* in fact has the right to choose the clan chief when a vacancy occurs. As I have said, the choice of the selecting subclan must be unanimous, and their choice must be acceptable to the rest of the clan, but here there is not the same demand for complete unanimity.

The ceremony at which a clan install their chief symbolizes this unity. Its three main parts are the 'blessing' of the chief (marking his forehead), his bathing, and obeisance to him. The first and third elements must involve three categories of people: the chiefs of every *perut* in the clan, the *anakbuah* (kin) ordinary members from each subclan, and finally the *seka*, elderly women representing the female members of the clan, again, at least one from each *perut*. Nowadays, at least, only a small proportion of the people included in these categories attends the ceremony, but the symbolism is clear—the participation of the whole clan in raising up the chief, and then recognizing his authority.

His installation by the clan is not in itself sufficient to make a chief. When they have selected and installed their choice the clan must then inform the *Undang*, through the Dato Mentri. If there is no valid, or strong, objection to the new chief from the *Undang*, or the Council of Eight, he will then be formally presented to the *Undang* by his clan. Only then will he become a properly appointed clan chief.

The objections raised against a proposed new chief should reflect either on his qualifications for the post, or his ability to perform it. Thus, a candidate is disbarred by a misdemeanour, whether his own, or his kin's, which has not been settled according to *adat*. Or the Dato Ombi may decide that the rules of rotation have not been properly followed. Madness, or serious illness, such as tuberculosis, would also disqualify.

But it often appears that the formal arguments advanced against a candidate are in fact excuses for personal objections. Faced with rumours of such opposition the *waris* may well retreat before they have installed their first choice and choose another more likely to be acceptable; perhaps the person on whose behalf the original objections were made. The election of a clan chief, and even more that of an *Undang*, give rise to much convassing and bribery to secure support from the *Undang* and the Council of Eight. Despite the right of a clan to choose its own chief the *Undang* can exercise much influence over the choice, especially as he can refuse to accept, or at least delay the acceptance of, a candidate he does not like.

What are the factors which influence the choice?

Hereditary entitlement is of prime importance. It must be established which subclan is entitled to provide the next chief, and that a candidate is a full member of that group, with his claim not weakened by any adoption in his genealogy, and that he does not belong to a branch debarred from holding office by a breach of *adat*. But elimination on such grounds may still leave a wide field for choice.

Attention now turns to a candidate's personal qualities. It will be a wealthier member of the group who is chosen. I have spoken of bribery as playing a part in the selection, but bribery has moral connotations which do not apply here. It is regarded as wrong to accept money from one person and then support another, but it is not wrong to give and receive presents in return for support in elections. Wealth is necessary if the chief is to live in a proper style, and not bring shame to his kin. A wealthy chief can give feasts when the appropriate occasions arise, without donations from the clan, and he can make fitting contributions at the feasts of others. Also he will not be tempted to dishonesty in matters affecting clan land when he gives advice to Magistrates in litigation affecting the ancestral property of his kin.

Wealth as a criterion of selection is particularly important under modern conditions, for now the only direct economic perquisites of office are small political pensions of between $20.00 and $35.00 a month, and such sums are not sufficient to cover the expenses of a chief who takes his duties seriously.

Economic position is however a more general criterion of status, and perhaps to say that the wealthy are chosen is to say little more than that the chiefs are chosen from amongst the important members of the clan.

A man's relations with his female kin may be a point of importance. Clan ceremonies are carried out in the chief's mother's or sister's house, for a man belongs in the house of his female kin rather than his wife's, although he may well have built the latter. In at least one case informants explained the failure of a man, with otherwise excellent qualifications, to secure clan office by his lack of female kin nearer than second cousin; a connection too remote to give him any strong claim to make frequent use of their house, with the attendant disruption of ordinary family life, and the extra work which feasts and continual visitors involve.

These objective qualifications do not exhaust the factors deciding an election. A man's character and conduct also play a part. But these are qualities which elude rigorous discussion. It is also difficult to predict the outcome of the ramifications of positive and negative influence, and of paternal and affinal connections, outside a particular case.

As an illustration I will discuss a dispute which started in late 1954.

A had emerged as the strong preference of the clan. B, his sister's husband was a *lembaga* in the Council of Eight. This would seem to give A a strong chance of being favourably received when presented to the *Undang*, and the *waris* accordingly proceeded with the installation ceremony which took place in B's house. But A was not received by the *Undang*, and it emerged that B was among the strongest of the Eight in opposing A, or at least, in supporting the *Undang* in his dislike of A.

Under matrilineal *adat* the relations between a man and his sister's husband are often strained, but in this case there was no history of disagreement to presage this hostility, and such overt action against one's wife's kin (*tempat semanda*) is a serious *adat* offence. A clan chief is less subject than other men to the authority of his wife's kin, but in the past such behaviour would have left no alternative but divorce, for a *lembaga*'s dignity would not allow him to make the necessary compensatory sacrifice to restore good relations.

In explaining B's behaviour it is necessary first to note his close relations with the *Undang*; secondly, and this was stressed by A's supporters, B's son had been elected *ibubapa* to replace A on his promotion. It was said that B hoped that if there were sufficient opposition to A, and the *waris* withdrew their support from him, his son would have a chance of becoming *lembaga*. This plot was certainly not successful, for it simply resulted in the *perut* replacing the son with another man loyal to A.

In this illustration the *waris* resisted the *Undang*'s attempt to choose their chief for them. The strength of this resistance derives, at least in part, from the pride of the *waris silasila* in their special position. But a clan may well not be able to unite in opposition to the *Undang*, especially if some members were halfhearted in their support of the proposed candidate, and may either compromise and propose the candidate known to be preferred, or, if any sort of unity cannot be achieved, allow the choice to go to the *Undang*.

To be married to a woman from outside the *luak*, even if she were living in it, would weigh against a candidate, and informants said that a man would have to take a local wife to be considered. Here we have to rely on conjecture. A man married to a foreign woman would not possess influential affinal ties, and so would probably not be considered as a candidate.

Any holder of office, no matter how minor, is automatically dismissed if he moves out of the *luak*.

OTHER MAJOR GROUPS

The relations of the eight clans and the *Undang* provided the basic structure of the traditional polity, but there remain a number of other important elements to be discussed.

Two of the major clans have divisions whose chiefs are not members of the Council of Eight. The first of these is a division of the *waris* Sarin, under Dato Raja-di-Raja, who are excluded from succession to the chieftainship of the *waris* Sarin because the first Dato Raja had a man executed without referring the case to the *Undang*. The second is a division of the *waris* Mungkal under

Dato Bandar. This group, who are known as the clan of the water (*waris di-ayer*), formerly had the right to collect dues on river traffic (now non-existent). The presence of this minor clan is the sole trace in Jelebu of the major division in Rembau and Sungei Ujong referred to above.

Another interesting group are the *waris* Tiga Batu, the matrilineal kin (*ayer kaki*) of the former Yam Tuan Muda of Jelebu. This royal line stems from Raja Adil, sometimes said to have been a younger brother of Raja Melewar, the first ruler of Negri Sembilan, established in Jelebu at the request of the people that they be given a *raja* to live amongst them.

As in Sri Menanti, the history of royalty in Jelebu is violent and confused, and complicated by the question of the *Raja*'s rights relative to the *Undang* and the clan chiefs. The *Raja* continually attempted to arrogate to himself rights jealously guarded by the *adat* chiefs who were not prepared to allow him any concrete power, but rather wished him to depend on them for everything. The struggle was only resolved when the Yam Tuan Mudaship was abolished after the British decided to support the *Undang*. In addition, the chief of the *waris* Tiga Batu, who stood in much the same relation to the *Raja* as the Mentri to the *Undang*, was no longer recognized as one of the *lembaga* of the *luak*. The community still exists at Kampong Batu Serambai, the *pusaka* of not only the *waris* Tiga Batu, but also of many *Tengku* and *Raja*.

There are also attached subclans, and groups of foreigners incorporated as such in the *adat* system.

Attached subclans arose through the immigration of groups of Malays from outside the *luak* in the days when the *adat* was still operative. The saying is 'the boat has a mooring, and the foreigner his fixed place'. Unless attached in some way to the kinship organization the foreigner is an outlaw, with no one to protect him, or to answer for his wrongdoings. Since a male immigrant leaves no kin at his death the quasi-adoption of *anak angkat*, whereby he would be treated by local people as a son but without any formal change in status and no rights to succession or inheritance, would suffice. But where the immigrants included women an arrangement had to be made which would provide a place not only for them but for their descendants. The newcomers would become relatives (*kadim*) to Jelebu people.

Two ways of effecting this may be distinguished, the choice

between them apparently depending on the numbers to be absorbed. If the newcomers were many a formal relationship would be created at clan level. In return for payment of a knife, cooking pot and a piece of cloth, the immigrants would be given a *pusaka*. They would be given land, to be held as other clan lands are held, and an office, the holder of which would function as *ibubapa* for his group. The newcomers were not, however, included in the succession to major clan offices.

Smaller groups were integrated through agreement between individuals, although this must imply the consent of the clan, for succession to land and office were involved. Giving examples informants remarked, 'my grandmother took their grandmother as sister'.

Besides foreigners integrated into existing kin-groups there are chiefs for people from Rembau, Pahang and Pilah, in Malaya, and Minangkabau, Jambi and Java in Indonesia. The largest group of Indonesian migrants in Jelebu, Mandahiling Batak, have no place in the *adat* system at all. They settled in numbers at the turn of the century, and even then the old arrangements were beginning to decay.

A SUMMARY OF THE 'CUSTOM LAW'

Knowledge of the 'custom law' is greatest where it concerns property, for this was retained under the British administration. Even today there are limitations on the devolution and sale of ancestral land (*tanah pusaka*), restricting the rights of individuals in accordance with the *adat* rules, although these rules are now administered by magistrates.

Property fell into two categories, inherited and acquired. In each category the most important item was land. As the law now operates all ancestral land is owned by women, and passes on death to daughters in equal shares. If one daughter dies before receiving her share, that share should go to her daughters to be divided amongst them. Where a woman has no daughters her land is inherited by her classificatory daughters, in the first place her sister's daughters (*anak sanak ibu*), failing them by women descended from her mother's sisters, and so on. The people say that the women have always owned the land, but it is certain that such ownership was formerly much limited by the rights of male kin to support, and their control of their sisters and sisters' children.

Rights to sell land were severely restricted. Almost the only legitimate reason for sale was to meet obligations to male kin. Sale was also subject to the prior option of kin to purchase. First near kin, then, should they not wish to buy, members of the same *perut*, then members of the same clan.

Control over these inherited lands was exercised by the chiefs. Apart from specific rules about inheritance and sale, an individual's rights of ownership were restricted by the notion that all land was the inheritance of the clan and the subclan, and so, in a way, of the group as a whole, as well as of the individuals owning it at any particular time. Besides ensuring that the rules were followed, control of land also implied a less well-defined task of ensuring that the land was properly used.

When *adat* was at its strongest the land in individual possession was nearly all riceland and homestead, for Jelebu seems to have been too remote to have participated in developments such as the early cultivation of pepper in Rembau. Even with these types of land there was no shortage.

The ancestral land of a clan included large areas of jungle, not allocated for individual use, although an individual or group might be able to establish a claim to some fruit trees. It was this abundance of land which made it possible to accept migrants, and give them land, for only a token payment. *Adat* divides this clan land into two types. The lands of the *biduanda* acquired by inheritance are called *tanah ta'tebus* (unredeemed land), while the lands of the other three clans, having been bought from the *biduanda*, are *tanah tebus* (redeemed land). As the redeemed lands were held in perpetuity the distinction is really only a reflection of the superior prestige position of the *biduanda*.

If a woman owns more land than she needs, she should allow her kin to use it without payment, or for a token only, 'for the land was their grandmothers' too'. This would not affect the devolution of the land.

Acquired property might be freely disposed of during the lifetime of the owner, but with death passed into the category of ancestral property. (The rule concerning automatic change to inherited property was changed under the British. An individual might register acquired property as ancestral land if he so wished, in which case the restrictions would apply. Recently even this rule was changed, and now no more land may be placed in the category *tanah pusaka*.)

There is a major distinction between property acquired by a single person (*charian bujang*) and that acquired by a married couple (*charian laki-bini*). The latter is joint property and must be divided on divorce, or at the death of one partner.

Property brought to the marriage by the man is *harta pembawa*, and by the woman *harta dapatan*. At marriage the assets of the spouses must be declared before the *ibubapa*. Any item of property not declared is assumed to have been part of the *charian laki-bini*.

A man's rights in kin property were very restricted. Should he plant trees on clan land the trees and their produce were his. In case of need he might be allowed to use a piece of kin land during his lifetime, but in no case could he dispose of it and at his death it should revert to the previous owner. A man might be allowed to inherit items of strictly male use, such as clothing and weapons, but even here there was no absolute right, but rather a sentimental recognition of the ties between kin.

While unmarried (whether as a youth, after divorce or as a widower) a man was entitled to support from his female kin. The *perut* were responsible for personal debts, and for two other categories of debt: debts of inheritance, *hutang pusaka*, and debts of custom, *hutang adat*. The former included marriage expenses (including fines for irregular marriages), and payments towards the pilgrimage and religious education. Debts of custom were the many fines which the holder of *adat* office might incur, for he bore responsibility for the actions of the whole group.

Even today informants speak of a man with many sisters as 'having an easy time', and within living memory it was possible for a man to make continual demands on his sisters, in which their husbands must either acquiesce, seeing the wealth they had helped accumulate disappear, or divorce their wives, for to restrain the brother-in-law would have constituted an offence against the *tempat semanda*, and have cost a reconciliation feast without achieving anything.

Nearly all *adat* law is concerned with maintaining good relations between groups, with a fine for the guilty, compensation for the injured, and a reconciliation feast given by the wrongdoer to the wronged. Only breach of the exogamy rules, and infringements of the prerogatives of the *Undang* were offences of a really public character. But even a minor offence, if not quickly settled, might develop into an infringement of the *Undang*'s prerogatives, for a chief who did not settle a wrongdoing amongst his kinsmen was in turn guilty of that offence at the next highest level as the responsible representative of his kin.

The fine was paid to the chief settling the case. To whom a case was taken was partly determined by the relationship of the parties. If they were members of the same *perut* then it would go first to the *ibubapa*. If the parties were members of different clans the case would probably reach the *Undang* quickly for there would be no chief of lower status with control over both. Of importance also were the intrinsic seriousness of the offence, the weight given it by the offended, and the obstinacy in refusing settlement of the offenders. The fines imposed by the *Undang* were larger and his feasts had to be larger too. For a case settled by an *ibubapa* a goat was the feast item, for a *lembaga* one buffalo, and two for the *Undang*, with correspondingly greater quantities of rice and other items.

In their judgements the *lembaga* were very much limited by *adat*, and if they exceeded their rights they would be guilty, in turn, of an offence against the *Undang*. The *Undang* on the other hand, was recognized as possessing much greater freedom in the exercise of his authority, a necessary power if he were to be able to settle cases brought to an impasse by differences in the interpretation of *adat*.

CHAPTER III

The Nature of the Economy

The preceding discussion of the traditional political system was primarily intended to provide the necessary setting for an understanding of contemporary social processes. In the same way the description of village economic organization which follows is mainly concerned with the social relations of economic actors as part of the total social organization rather than with pure economics.

A major feature of Redfield's distinction between peasant and folk society is that in the former the economy is more clearly distinguished from other aspects of the society than it is in the latter. The folk society defines a limited number of roles very broadly, so that instead of economic, political, religious and other types of roles, it is more useful to speak of such aspects of the major, usually kinship, roles. In the peasant society it is possible to see the recognition of economic roles defining a standard of expected behaviour independent of other relations between the individuals concerned. The separation is not complete because the household is the basic economic unit in both production and consumption. But there is still a sector of the social system which may be regarded as forming a limited system of economic roles.

In the above sense the Malay economy qualifies as peasant. The obligations of a rice cultivator to participate in collective irrigation work, or to maintain his fields so that no damage will result to other people's crops, fall to anyone cultivating a piece of land. People have many economic relations with relatives, and informants explained their behaviour as affected by these kinship ties, although not as a direct expression of kinship roles. In economic affairs kinship causes divergences from normal economic relations. People even speak as if they preferred to avoid economic relations with kin as far as possible, because of the obligation not to calculate carefully and to be generous. There is an extremely close connection between kinship and economic roles, but it is a connection. At the level of structure they are distinguished, although closely intertwined at the level of social organization where the individual has to reconcile all his various role obligations.

SUBSISTENCE AND PURCHASE

If necessary the peasant can meet many of his consumption needs through subsistence production. Traditional subsistence techniques are still known and can be revived if required, although these skills will get increasingly rarer as the present older generation dies. But subsistence production is second choice. The peasant concentrates on cash production, and the higher his money income the less he will find for himself in the village and the jungle. He does not even try to become self-sufficient in everyday necessities such as peppers, vegetables and coconuts, all of which would grow readily on the ample homestead which surrounds most houses.

The variable which determines the amount of subsistence production is the price of rubber. When this is buoyant the peasant abandons the plots for domestic consumption he made during a period of depressed prices. On the day that I arrived in Malaya the newspapers jubilantly announced that the price of rubber had reached 60 cents per lb. for the first time since the depression after the Korean War. During the following years prices were good, for much of the time near $1.00 per lb. Vegetable plots and fences which were tended when I first arrived have now been abandoned completely.

At any given time the wealthy will rely less on subsistence production than the poor, buying not only more goods but a wider variety. They eat bought vegetables while the poor collect theirs, and buy, for example, mats and thatch, while the poor make their own. The exception to this rule is the cultivation of rice. Self-sufficiency in rice is very highly valued. If rice supplies are adequate until the next harvest, then, whatever happens, the peasant feels that he will survive somehow. Accordingly, a wealthy peasant who could well buy rice will seriously cultivate his fields, and it is not unfitting for the wife of a schoolteacher or a clerk, should she be living in her own village, to work her fields, and even for her husband to help her. Even so, an increasing number of peasants, especially in the vicinity of towns, are prepared to buy rice and concentrate on rubber production, a state of affairs known as 'rubber madness' (*gila getah*) to those self-righteous peasants who have not yet succumbed to it.

THE RURAL MALAY IN THE MALAYAN ECONOMY

Rural Malay society exports primary products to the rest of Malaya and imports consumption goods. All economic functions other than primary production are carried on by other races, above all by the Chinese. Rubber is sold as unsmoked sheet, often not even properly dried. Fruit and rice are sold at the road-side. Malays do not even have a place in the simple marketing and processing of their primary products.

The handling of consumer goods only comes into Malay hands, if at all, at the very last stage of the supply process, in the village shop. Even then the villagers buy many of their needs direct from the neighbouring town. They have to go there to sell their rubber, and goods there are more varied, cheaper, and of better quality than the limited stale stocks of the village shop. Malays are always willing to try shopkeeping and trading. Malay civilization was, after all, very much a trading one, but shops and other ventures normally fall victim to the Malay desire to, as they say, 'get rich all at once', and to bad debts.

A position of economic inferiority of one group within a country, or of one country amongst the nations, easily becomes institutionalized, or self-perpetuating, illustrating Myrdal's (1957, pp. 11 ff.) 'circular and cumulative causation process'. The argument is obviously applicable to the position of the Malays in Malaya, but by itself seems to imply that poverty is sufficient to explain poverty or backwardness, and that, if the positions were reversed, those countries or groups now poor, if made rich, would stay rich and get richer, and those now rich, if made poor, would stay poor and get poorer. Such an explanation is in danger of underestimating the possibility that there are relevant differences between groups and countries which affect their economic success apart from their relative economic positions. One such area of difference may be the attitudes and values concerning economic activity, for these have important implications for economic activity through motivation. Differences in this respect are very marked between Malays and Chinese in Malaya (Swift, 1962).

Malays often explain their relative failure in economic activity by claiming that they, unlike other races, are not obsessed with base things like money, but are attracted by finer things and feelings, pointing to the importance of Islam for the Malay, and asking 'where have the Chinese any religion?' Now if the Malay can be shown to be markedly ascetic or otherworldly, this would have obvious economic implications which would go far to explain his economic failure when compared with the Chinese.

The Malay does not, however, give any impression of being unconcerned with wealth, or markedly less so than the Chinese, as far as his expressed attitudes and desires are concerned. The villagers show a very great desire for modern consumption goods, and to be rich, and their conversations reveal that they feel deprived because they cannot obtain such goods, and envious of those who can. What is marked is not a difference in the desire for wealth between the two races, but a difference in the meaning wealth has for them.

The Chinese view is essentially long term. Wealth is desired not only for consumption but for accumulation, to build up a fortune which can be handed on to future generations. This attitude is obviously in keeping with the importance of the lineage in Chinese culture. The stress on the importance of both ancestors and descendants to the living must mean a minimization of the importance of the present. Present sacrifice in the interest of future prosperity is well worth while, whether it takes the form of extra work, extra worry and foresight, or of abstinence from consumption, to build up capital.

By contrast the Malay is interested in the short run. Wealth is strongly desired, but for consumption. Potential future benefit is not weighed highly against present sacrifice. The rational course of economic action seeking to maximize satisfaction must differ with the period of calculation. The Malay preference for the short run is not, in itself, uneconomic or irrational, but it does make for weakness in economic competition with groups or individuals with a long run orientation.

A marked fatalism, presented in religious form, is also conspicuous among Malay economic attitudes. The Malay is very prone, after receiving a setback, to give up striving, and say that he has no luck, that it is the will of God. In economic affairs this is most clearly seen in the concept *rezeki*, a person's divinely determined economic lot. *Rezeki* may bring rewards which seem unearned by earthly standards, or deny them when they would seem fully deserved.

The Chinese is very superstitious in the weight given to super-natural factors in economic matters. But this is a magical attitude. Supernatural assistance will be sought from whatever source seems likely to be efficacious, and if one does not work another is tried, while all the while the human does not desist from his own efforts to achieve the desired result. For the Malay there is no way of altering one's fate. A good magician may be able to con-trol the spirits, but behind the spirits there is God, who has written every destiny, and whose purposes are beyond human understanding, let alone control. This is to point a consistency between beliefs and attitudes in the fields of religion and econ-omics and not to claim a causal standing for either of them.

A further consistency exists, I feel, between these two fields and that of the socialization of the individual within the family. I assume that consistency of reward and punishment in early childhood produces a personality which 'needs' to perform well according to parental expectations. Such a personality in later life may be expected to show just those qualities of compulsive drive and striving which the Malay lacks. And in the Malay home, the pattern of discipline, of reward and punishment of the child is not consistent. A child soon learns that tantrums are the most effective means of getting what it wants. But even here there is no certainty. Adults may pamper the child, usually bribing it to stop its tantrum. Or the child may be ignored completely, while its screams get fiercer and fiercer, and it stamps more and more furiously on the floor. Or it may be punished, pinching or con-finement being preferred to slapping. An act of naughtiness may call forth either a scolding or a laugh, 'children will be children' *budak-budak-lah*. Nor can goodness be relied on to produce praise or a show of affection, for the good child is likely to be ignored, not being a problem needing attention at the moment. Affection is not necessarily earned by good conduct, nor lost by bad. I suggest that the observable features of Malay child care are connected with the equally observable tendency to see only a loose con-nection between reward and effort in economic affairs (through *rezeki*), or in life generally (through *takdir' llah* God's will).

The villagers attach great importance to security, in the sense of a desire to achieve a guaranteed minimum level of consumption which will not be risked for potential future gain. The peasant is reluctant to undertake ventures which will interfere with his existing economic arrangements. This attitude towards security helps to explain the attraction of employment with the Government, or other large employers, where the security of a fixed income compensates for the low wages.

It also helps to explain the peasant's approach to innovation, and to specialization within the village economy. The most important economic specialization is that between owner and tenant (or sharer). But even here both parties will probably be performing similar activities. They differ in their relation to the means of production rather than in occupation. Every peasant 'landlord' fit to work engages in agricultural activity. It is true that some of them do not tap rubber, but this is largely a matter of age specialization. They tapped when they were younger, and even poor elderly men, who need the income, struggle along without tapping.

Specialization, in the sense of carrying on an occupation which others do not, is very limited, a reflection of the place of the Malays in the Malayan economy. Most markedly different are the wage-earning representatives of the modern official class living in the village, and the few villagers engaged in menial work for the Government, either locally or in the town. The former are very important in village society but neither category of wage-earner is really of the village economy. Their incomes are derived from outside, and their consumption expenditure, like that of other Malays, goes very quickly into the hands of the Chinese. Where the wage-earner may be important for the village economy is in using his savings to accumulate village property.

Religious specialists (*orang alim* or *lebai*) are also a special category. Those fortunate enough to have salaried positions in schools approximate very closely to secular school teachers in both status and outlook. But not all of them are so fortunate. The *imam* of a mosque is not a fulltime specialist, nor is the *mudin* who carries out circumcisions. The 'charity' they receive at feasts, and presents from the parents of their Koran pupils, are important for the *lebai* but rarely will this income be sufficient for them to stop village work entirely. A *lebai* may not tap rubber, but at least he and his wife will grow rice.

Other specialists are the craftsmen who can do simple carpentry, or sewing, or cut hair. These men never make a full time specialism of their craft, although a very few may approach this. They are, it is true, subject to strong competition from the Chinese in town, but preference for a fellow Malay, their ties with the villagers who are their potential customers, and the fact that they work in the village with low overheads, give them an advantage as long as they do not aspire to town premises. It is the fear of insecurity which precludes full time specialization. Craftsmen say they dare not devote all their time to their craft because they would then have to abandon village work altogether, and have nothing to fall back on. This attitude is partly explained by lack of capital. Having little or nothing in reserve they need a regular flow of income, and cannot withstand a slack period, while the other villagers' expenditure on clothes and houses fluctuates seasonally. Nor can they undertake enough work to spread the risk of late payment and default as can the larger town business which employs labourers. A Malay must pay cash for his supplies and equipment since he has neither the reputation, nor the ties with a (Chinese) merchant, which would make him credit-worthy. But the craftsman's fear is also a self-fulfilling prophecy; because he is frightened there will not be enough business he loses business. As the Malay is not always available some villagers prefer to do business with a Chinese and be sure that he will not be late finishing a piece of work because he has had to complete his rice planting first. I have seen an initially flourishing tailor fail in this way. The villagers said his work was good, his prices satisfactory, and they liked to help a Malay, relative and neighbour, but they could never be sure when they would get their completed cloth back. A carpentry shop operated by three men was not a failure, but was not as flourishing as it might have been. The men were capable of good work, and two of them were in fact employed by the Government. After finishing their wage labour at 2 p.m. each day, they began work in their shop, where they were joined by the third man, who tapped rubber in the morning. They were more often turning away work, or annoying customers by not finishing a job on the agreed date, than slack, but the two wage-earners dared not take the risk of leaving the security of their morning employment, although the return from full-time employment in their workshop would have been higher.

Young Malay men desire to leave the village and work for

wages. An announcement that one of the Services is recruiting will cause hundreds of youths from all over the State to go to Seremban, although few of them have the requisite educational qualifications, and fewer still will be accepted. All my young friends in the village had written applications to one or other of the Services. It was not that they were particularly martial, but that they could see no other opportunity. The period when anyone might get a job in the Forces ended with the easing, and then the conclusion of the Emergency.

MIXED ECONOMY

The Malay economy of Jelebu is an example of a type found widely throughout Central Malaya based on the production of three major crops, rice, rubber and fruit, although also carrying on a wide range of other minor activities. The presence of several major sources of income is of great importance for the economy, and differentiates it from that of the inhabitants of the northern alluvial plains, dependent wholly on rice, from the east-coast fishermen, or from the copra growers of many coastal areas.

A second feature of the economy is that land is not yet in seriously short supply. This is a generalization difficult to substantiate for the area as a whole, for land shortage is not solely a matter of land : population ratio. Some Malay communities near towns, in areas of large estates, or whose land was suitable for tin-mining, are short of land. Typically land use is extensive throughout this central area with villages bordered by waste lands and jungle which might be cultivated. At least as far as Jelebu is concerned, besides the opening of new jungle land there was also a certain amount of 'slack' in the use of land already alienated. At any moment there were always a few rubber lots without tappers, or lots not fully tapped which might be subdivided. There were rice plots which their owners would as soon rent out as cultivate themselves were there anyone prepared to rent them. *Kampong* land is hardly cultivated at all, and many lots under tree crops could certainly be more intensively planted.

Relative abundance of land is not a permanent feature of the economy. Population growth is continuous and large, and my figures do not include many families absent with the Security Forces. Unless the Government's land development schemes make more impact than they had done at the time of study, or new avenues for employment away from the land are soon opened up, an increasing shortage of land must be expected.[1]

[1] Much higher prices for land were reported when I made a very brief visit to Jelebu in September 1963, suggesting that my prediction is being fulfilled.

CHAPTER IV

The Major Products: Rice

Rice is mainly grown as a subsistence contribution to household consumption. All Malay villages in Jelebu grow some rice, but few are able to meet all their needs from one harvest to the next, and even fewer can produce a surplus for sale. The major rice surplus area is the newly opened settlement area towards the Pahang border. There the land is still very fertile, holdings are large, and so far the peasants have no other sources of income competing with it for their attention. In the areas of older settlement around the district capital a surplus is much rarer. Only two small valleys always have a surplus larger than can be disposed of in intra-village transactions and sufficient to justify organized sale to a dealer or the Government.

Usually few people are obliged to buy rice until the last weeks before the harvest. However, the harvest is not always good, and even in a generally good year bad weather or pests may bring a poor crop to some small areas. Moreover, people who should have enough rice for their consumption needs may be tempted to sell after the harvest, although they know that later in the year they will have to find money to buy rice. Finally, some areas miss cultivation altogether.

My work was concentrated in one of the small surplus valleys. There, in an average year, no one need buy rice, unless he had sold more than he could spare, or had his calculations upset by a succession of unexpected feasts or prolonged visits from kin. Every year there was a surplus for outside sale.

THE OWNERSHIP OF LAND

Despite the weakening of *adat* the vast majority of rice holdings are still owned by women. A survey of the land register revealed that in 1955, of 157 titles registered in the 'downstream' half of the *mukim* only seven were held by men. (In the following discussion I will nevertheless refer to the rice land as if it were owned by the husband. The family is the economic unit, and formally at least the husband is the entrepreneur for that unit.)

This pattern of ownership cannot be attributed solely to the force of *adat* as law. Some rice land is not registered as ancestral property, although it is so according to *adat*, and is regarded as such by its owners. Other land, although registered as *pusaka*, can legally pass to a son if there is no daughter to inherit (even if there are *sanak-ibu* daughters), and if the magistrate and the *lembaga* who advises him on *adat* decide that it should (assuming such a devolution to be contested). In other cases I have found land, which other kin and neighbours assured me was *pusaka*, registered under ordinary title. Informants were sure that a son could inherit, and although I did not observe a case which enabled me to test this view, there is no doubt about the present view of what should occur.

A man may also buy rice land. This he can do when someone needs to sell, and there are no near kin of the owner wishing to exercise an option, or when the land is already the property of his or his wife's kin. In bargaining about land sales the question of kinship is continually raised. The intending buyer stresses that he is 'not a stranger', and other people talking about the sale discuss whether the buyer is a proper person to receive the land, and whether the sale will harm members of the *perut*.

If a man buys either rice land or *kampong* he cannot register it in his own name without seeming to be planning to divorce his wife. He is also obliged to provide a portion for his daughter on marriage.[1] Not all fathers can do this, but it is a general aim. It would once have been the duty of the subclan to provide a portion of the kin property for each newly adult woman member, with which she might raise her family.

Matrilocal marriage makes for the retention of this pattern of female ownership, especially while rice growing is regarded as a woman's task. And there is little quarrel with matrilocality. Even a father who wishes he could retain a son to help with his property recognizes that no family will allow a daughter to go and live with her husband's kin, nor would he allow his own daughters to do so. Furthermore, the strong mother-daughter tie found

---

[1] The saying concerning a daughter's portion is '*nyior sa-batang, sawah sa-lopak, kampong sa-sudut*'. A coconut tree, a piece of riceland and a corner of the homestead.

everywhere in Malay society supports matrilocality where it is already an institutionalized pattern.

A generation ago lots of five to six acres were common, and 'every one' kept buffalo to cultivate this large area. Division has now so reduced holdings that a lot of about one acre is the most common. If carefully tended such a field will provide subsistence for a household of husband, wife and children, but another generation will see many holdings too small for family subsistence.

There is no great desire to grow more rice than is needed for food. For most families rice money is not something planned for and relied on. Only for the aged and for single women is rice an essential source of cash. It is also important, although relatively less so, since it provides a much smaller proportion of their total income, to the wealthy, men who regularly produce a surplus. People who have more land than they need for subsistence are disposed to rent it out.

Compared with other forms of village work rice growing is not an unprofitable activity. Assuming that all rice grown is sold at the 1959 guaranteed price of $15.00 a pikul, and assuming reasonably fertile land, an acre should yield at least $120.00 for what should not be more than a month's work, although it will be spread over a much longer period. This compares well with the $40.00 to $60.00 which an industrious share-tapper may hope to receive in a tapping month of 20 days. But rice growing interferes with rubber tapping, which is man's work and provides the regular income for consumption needs. Also the planting, which is women's work, is an onerous burden for a mother with young children. She will manage what must be done, but beyond that the disutility of labour becomes greater than the additional return.

With regard to renting land the situation is as follows. Some people with less land than they need to meet subsistence requirements are willing to rent land to make up this deficiency in their food supply. Other people have more land than they need for subsistence, which they find a burden to work, but can still manage to cultivate. However they do not seek tenants. A man whose wife owns land in the village but who is working elsewhere may find that he cannot get rent for it. If the land is not cultivated he will be summoned, so he will be pleased to get anyone to work it. But it is usually the would-be tenant who looks for land.

Tenancy agreements between people who are not closely related rarely survive many harvests. Even a man who regularly rents changes his landlord frequently, and the man who always rents out land frequently changes his tenants. Even when there is no open disagreement there is a mild tension in the relationship, as if the tenant begrudged paying the owner of the soil any of the produce of his labour, while the landlord regrets that anyone else should share the produce of his land.

Renting by close relatives is a different matter. A man with more land than he needs is under strong pressure to allow his wife's poor relatives to use it. The land is their inheritance too; it belonged to their grandmother as well as his wife's. If a man wishes to avoid the accusation that he is getting rich by using his wife's *pusaka*, and to keep on good terms with his wife's kin, whose assistance he will probably one day need, he must be generous in matters affecting them. Renting arrangements between close kin persist year after year. Kin are charged a smaller rent than outsiders, and it is often spoken of as a token, although it is more than a nominal payment. Also a relative can plead special circumstances to justify not paying some or all of the rent without the agreement being terminated.

Rents are fixed by general opinion of what is just. One hundred bushels of unhusked rice per acre, or a third of the crop, is regarded as reasonable, and rents in fact approach this norm. A piece of land that is hard to work or irrigate will be cheaper. Informants also suggested that an especially good piece of land would be worth more, but they were not able to give any instances.

Village ideas make a bargain conditional on the circumstances. When these change the person whose condition is worsened feels entitled to a revision of the bargain. The other party will probably not willingly accept the need for change, but there exist no mechanisms within the village by which he can enforce the original bargain. Appeal to outsiders, such as the *Penghulu* (the official in charge of a *mukim*), is normally out of the question, for such an action will place the complainant in the wrong whatever the popular opinion on the original facts of the case. The informal pressures of public opinion and shame will not help either, for they will favour a reasonable adjustment of the bargain. This attitude to bargains and obligations introduces a great element of uncertainty into village economic calculations, which must operate as a bar to economic progress.

With rice rents the tenant in a bad year may pay less than the agreed sum to the owner, and in an especially good year might give a little more. The landlord is more or less obliged to accept what he is given. He can only apply the sanction of terminating the agreement, and this will not seriously harm the tenant.

An indication of the frequency of tenancy may be derived from the fact that in 1955, of 38 cultivating units 7 were tenants. Three of these had made agreements with close kin; the others had no direct ties with their landlords. The three kin tenants' agreements had lasted for some years, and two of them are still (1960) in existence. In 1956, of 40 cultivating units 9 were renters, and apart from the three kin bargains all the others were either new tenants or had changed landlords. (These figures refer to the cultivators using one irrigation system, the major part of the population of one village, but not all of it, and including outsiders as tenants.)

STAGES OF PRODUCTION

Only one crop of rice is grown each year following seasons suited to the rainy periods of September, a mildly rainy period, and December, when the monsoons bring heavy rains. The seasonal variations in climate are not so marked as to make cultivation outside the season impossible, but sufficient to make it desirable to follow the conventional timetable.

The main phases of the production cycle are as follows:

Naik ayer: Build dam and repair irrigation channels. June.
Menyankol and *membalek:* Hoeing and the preparation of the soil for planting. June, July, August and September.
Menyemai: Preparation of seedling nurseries and the planting of seed. Late July or August.
Mengubah: The transplanting of seedlings. September.
Meremput: Weeding and anti-pest activities which are carried on sporadically throughout the growing season.
Menuai: Harvest. February.

It will be noted that while the actual growing period is only six months the work is spread over nine. This is because it is done intermittently, especially the heaviest task of preparing the fields. At any time during the period there will be some individuals working in the fields, but only towards the end of this phase, when the time for planting approaches, will most cultivators go regularly to their fields.

Naik ayer

This activity only takes place in villages where the people still manage their own irrigation. An increasing number of villages rely on Government supplies of irrigation water.

After every harvest the fields are used for pasture, and the irrigation works inevitably suffer much damage. The dam itself is broken shortly before the harvest to allow the fields to dry. The first work of the rice year is therefore to repair all the channels and rebuild the dam. The dam itself, and the upper reaches of the irrigation channel which do not run by or through any fields, are repaired communally, every cultivating family being obliged to provide one worker.

The first question is when to build the dam. The seasonal timetable allows a wide measure of variation, as does the Government timetable which seeks to impose uniformity over the District. Much depends on the decision of the village leaders, but two general considerations may be noted. The fasting month is determined by the lunar calendar, and is therefore moveable in terms of the solar, which is also the rice calendar. As far as possible people avoid all major tasks during the fasting month. The second consideration is the experience of the previous year. If this had been difficult, for example if the dam had broken several times and the water shortage had delayed cultivation, or if the villagers had been too leisurely and were then forced to hurry, they will tend to go to the other extreme the following year. On the other hand, if the year before they had found themselves ahead of other villages, so that they were forced to delay work and allow weeds the chance to spring up again, they will proceed more slowly.

The first individual task of the rice year is for each person to ensure that his plot's irrigation channels are clear and watertight. Otherwise water will not reach the downstream fields, and this will cause much bad feeling.

The method of irrigation used for all Malay works in Jelebu is to divert a stream into a drainage channel running alongside the valley floor. From this channel water is let off at intervals into the fields and thence flows back to the river bed. The hilly topography, and the abundance of streams, make this a simple irrigation method presenting few technical problems. Each holding must be divided into small plots with raised boundaries so as to spread the water over the whole field. There is enough water for all as long as no-one takes more water than he needs.

The necessary cooperative work can be completed in two or three hours. Even this work is not intense, and while some people work hard, others do very little at all. There is little organization; no leader takes it upon himself to tell others what to do. Everyone knows what must be done; the leader is the man who throws himself most energetically into the task, and thereby forces others to follow his lead.

The dam is only made of branches, stones and earth. A heavy rain storm may sweep it away. Should the damage be extensive the whole group is mobilized as for the original construction, but minor repairs are usually done by someone who notices the water level falling and does not want his fields to dry up.

In the Malay view dams do not break often by chance. Should breakages be frequent there is suspicion of supernatural malevolence or irritation. The river has a spirit, and so has each plot of rice land. Rice too has a spirit. A good crop depends on the good will of these beings. There was once a well developed system of belief and ritual connected with rice, but this no longer survives in well-organized form. There is no standard body of knowledge: some people know more than others, and people know different things. Also most people know more than they practise.

In the area where this study was concentrated all the villagers participated in a ceremony to placate the spirits and ensure their assistance in getting a good crop. The village magician (*pawang*) chose the day. This was usually a Sunday, as the villagers were proud of their ceremony and liked to invite Government officials to attend. Every family took to the dam offerings of glutinous rice coloured with saffron, and hard-boiled eggs. The contribution of each family was partly determined by its wealth and status, but each plot of land had a traditional offering which was called the *adat* of the plot, the payment promised each year to its guardian, and made the following year at this ceremony, where a further promise would be made (*niat*). In addition one family always offered a large construction of saffron rice (*nasi gedang*) which occupied a place of honour in the celebrations.

Near the dam site the *pawang* placated the spirits with spells and offerings of food and incense. Having completed his work he announced the taboos for the following year. In 1955 he said that we might see a large fish swimming up the channel, and we must not interfere with it. He also forbade anyone to eat another variety of fish in the (unlikely) event of their catching one in the channel. The *adat* for his work was 42 c., but 'that is not money today', and the minimum agreed contribution was 5 c. per cultivator.

The ceremony is important to the villagers quite apart from the question whether they believe in it. They perform it, while neighbouring villages, which rely on the Government dam, do not. At the technical level the need to complete the dam before the ceremony can take place is an incentive to get the work finished. Less directly, the ceremony underlines the importance of rice and rice cultivation to the village, removing it from the level of an ordinary activity which anyone may carry out or not as he feels fit. If a man abandons his rubber holding he harms only himself; if he neglects his ricefield, he harms others. An argument can therefore be made for the functional value of magic as an expression of, and underpinning for, the moral value of rice cultivation. That this argument has weight is shown by the fact that this area has never been a problem for the administration. Every year, without threats or summons, or visits from the District Officer, the villagers carry on their cultivation in a way that compares very favourably with anything else the state can show.

But 'the possibility of experiment and invention is limited by their acceptance of a traditional system of magico-religious interpretations' (Firth, 1939, p. 91). In 1954 the dam broke four times in rapid succession, and each time was rebuilt. After the fifth breach the reaction of the villagers was that the *pawang* had failed to placate the spirits properly. They were resigned to losing their crop for the year. The village headman refused to accept this explanation, arguing that erosion, by altering the course of the stream, had made it undammable in the old way. On his own initiative he approached the District Office for cement and a large-bore pipe, and secured the assistance of the local Drainage and Irrigation Officer. He then cajoled the other villagers into helping him with the work, and bullied those adversely affected by the proposed new course into parting with their land. Together they redesigned the channel, using the pipe and cement for difficult stretches, and so managed to avoid further breakages at the weak spot. But for the headman's drive and his prestige, which disposed the Government to help him, the village would have been without rice for that year. The villagers' willingness to accept defeat cannot be blamed solely on magic. They would in any case have been disposed to give up after several failures, but magic was at least a validation of their attitude.

Menyankol and membalek

Baked by the sun, and trodden underfoot by cattle, the rice-fields become like stone during the fallow season. Grass, and in the damper parts tough weeds, spring up around the dead rice stalks. Before they can be planted the fields must be turned into smooth mud, completely clear of weeds.

Water has been let into the fields, and ankle deep the peasants carry on the most gruelling part of rice cultivation.

Even in a small country like Malaya there are several variations in method of rice cultivation, the choice between them depending on tradition, the nature of the soil, and the area to be cultivated. In Jelebu only two methods are used, hoe cultivation or working with a bull.

Ploughing with cattle is practised only by men, and mainly by the richer ones. A man who can afford not to tap rubber can spare the time to work in the ricefields, and can do so without fear for his prestige. Because of the heat cattle can be used only for a few hours in the morning, and this is the time when rubber tapping must be done, before the heat dries up the flow of latex. Rice cultivation must therefore be a secondary activity for the poor man. He may hoe a little in the afternoon, or when rain the previous night rules out tapping, but he will voluntarily stop tapping only if there is great need for haste in the ricefield.

The bull is used with two implements, a rake and a roller. These implements are made by the cultivators themselves from jungle wood.

Most peasants, both men and women, use a light, sharp hoe (*rembas*). Each plot is worked over with light clods cut from the soil and turned over so that the grass is covered. This is *menyankol*.[1] Because of the water mud will have formed, but it is still lumpy, therefore, shortly before planting the soil must be worked over again (*membalek*) to produce the desired consistency.

Attempts to calculate the necessary time of labour involved are frustrated by the irregular work habits of the villagers. Even the most industrious peasant does not work in his fields every day, or with uniform industry. They prefer to proceed slowly. The wife may work for an hour or two in the morning, while the husband does a little, on his own or with his wife, in the cool of the afternoon. Informants estimate that ten days would suffice for an acre of land 'if one really worked', and I am inclined to trust them in a matter which is their province, but it should be pointed out that this is hypothetical as no-one 'really works', in the sense of trying to complete cultivation in as short a time as possible to the exclusion of all other activities.

Menyemai

Seeds are first planted in nurseries, and are transplanted to the fields when they are twenty-eight days old. Although cultivators can name many varieties of rice which they grow, or used to grow, only two varieties are now widely planted. These, compared to the favoured Siamese rice of commerce, are hard and shortgrained, and are therefore difficult to sell outside the village, although they yield well under local conditions. Besides the rice planted for staple consumption some villagers plant small plots of glutinous rice (*pulut*) used for cakes and snacks.

A careful husbandman chooses his seeds well, but others will use any rice available. As an anthropologist I cannot judge the value of seed selection as practised by the peasants. Are the qualities which the grower seeks those which in fact will give a better yield? People who choose their seed carefully get higher yields, but they are also the people who are careful about all aspects of production. The selection of seed does however make for even ripening, and this is a great help towards efficient harvesting.

Nurseries are made on the jungle edge. A site is chosen where there is good soil, plentiful water, and little danger from pests.

[1] *Menyankol* to hoe, from *changkol* a heavy hoe which is, in fact, little used in rice cultivation. The use of the term was explained to me as a survival from the days when a wooden hoe was used to complete the bunds after cultivation by driving buffalo around the field.

It is therefore not necessary to fence and manure the plot, as it would be were it to be placed in the field. But in the fields the plots could be irrigated, and occasionally the seedlings die in a drought. This occurred throughout Negri Sembilan in 1954, and only emergency sales of seedlings by the Department of Agriculture enabled many peasants to plant at all.

Government propaganda stresses the advantage of irrigated nurseries, and the 1954 drought seemed to have made the point quite clearly. But in 1955 the peasants still made their nurseries on the traditional sites, despite much discussion during the year of changing to the recommended method. The Government's proposal was for communal nursery plots, which would facilitate fencing and manuring. But this presented organizational problems much greater than plans which the individual can carry out on his own. The new arrangements also required more work, and the peasantry were not entirely convinced that the change was necessary. Finally the women all opposed the plan because they said the seedlings were harder to pull up than in dry plots (they had tried the new method during the 'Japanese time'). The men stressed their wives' attitudes. They understood the new plan, but their wives did not, and after all, it was their wives' business.

Groups of sisters plant their seedlings together on portions of the same plot, returning to the same place year after year should it prove satisfactory. Since the work is done at the jungle's edge one or two of the husbands will go along for protection, but will not take part in the work.

Mengubah

About a month after the seeds are planted they must be moved to the fields. This is also women's work. First the nursery earth must be washed from the seedlings, and then they are thrust, three or four at a time, into the mud, until the whole field is covered with neat rows of seedlings. Untidy planting 'offends the eyes', and brings shame to the planter. Planting so many seedlings at a time is recognized as wasteful, but planting is intended to be a once and for all operation, without any need to go around later replacing dead seedlings.

An acre of land will occupy an industrious and skilful woman for three days of steady work. The seedlings must be planted before they get too old, and therefore there cannot be the same casualness here as in the other phases of rice work.

People begin their planting on a lucky day, placing an offering of seedlings in the centre of the plot before they start work. Lucky days are chosen on a personal basis. Everyone chooses a day in the waxing half of the moon, and Wednesday is ruled out altogether since it is the day of fire, a good day for clearing but not for planting. Each individual chooses a day that seems auspicious to him, say his birthday, or that of his child. If the actual work cannot be started on the chosen day, then placing the offering and planting a few seedlings will count.

Meremput

Every cultivator who wants to get a crop must carry out all the activities described so far. The activities I have gathered under the name *meremput* (grassing or weeding) are more optional, and it is here that the difference between the good and the careless cultivator will show. Conditions which favour rice also favour weeds, but the weeds will not endanger the actual life of the rice, so the cultivator who does not weed will still get some return. However weeding gives a higher return in aiding rice growth, lessening the depredations of rats and making the control of insect pests easier. Rat poison can be used, and is supplied by the Government, but so many deaths of (other people's) ducks result that many people prefer not to use it.

Fences require continual attention. Individual plots are not fenced but only the perimeter of the whole area. The fences are usually made of bamboo and rubber saplings. Cattle are restrained by the appearance of a fence but goats act as if a fence were a challenge. They persevere until they can force their bodies through, and if they are not stopped there is soon a hole which will allow the passage of cattle too, and cause a quarrel in the village. Finally irrigation channels must be continually inspected and repaired, for the flow of water is affected by erosion, and also by sediment which damages the crop if it is sandy.

All these activities do not take as much time as the earlier ones, but they call for continual attention. This is less trouble to the man who is not tapping rubber every day. Weeding also has a by-product in the grasses cut. During the growing season pasture is scarce, and owners are often forced to collect fodder for their beasts, so that it is sometimes difficult to tell which is the planter's main concern, weeding or fodder.

Aesthetic enjoyment of the appearance of the fields, and pride of ownership are further factors making for industry. The people who care for the appearance of their fields are also those who wish for a large crop, and to appear industrious. They say, we work hard, and we do such and such things, because it will increase the yield. But they also explain they would feel ashamed should their fields appear uncared for, and such people are also the most likely to express aesthetic appreciation of the fields and the crop, and to show supernatural concern for the spirit of the rice. This concern, although partly shown through rules which are presumably irrelevant to the success of the crop, also enjoins the reverent and careful carrying out of all phases of the cultivation cycle. All these factors support each other, and it is impossible to specify the particular contribution of each to the product.

Menuai

If the villagers are fortunate the rice will ripen evenly and quickly, but not all at once, so that it can be gradually harvested. The traditional method of harvesting is to cut each stalk separately just below the head of grain. Although the people are dextrous it is still a slow and laborious method, really advantageous only when the ripening is erratic, so that the ripe heads must be selected.

Another method is to cut armfuls of rice with a sickle, and beat out the grain on the side of a wooden, cloth-sided, box. This method can be used by a single individual, but it is quicker if one person beats the grain, while others cut the rice and bring it to him. It is therefore usual, even when a husband and wife are using the sickle, for them to revert to the traditional method when working separately. The traditional method is also used when labour is hired.

Recently (1956) there has been a minor technical revolution in the village where I was living. For the 1955 harvest only two harvesters used the sickle. In 1956 everyone used it at least part of the time. I cannot explain this sudden change. The villagers did not see that there was any problem. The new method was quicker and so they changed to it. Why had they not used it before? Some said they did not have the equipment; some did not know why. Imitative enthusiasms of this kind can catch on very quickly. I have seen, for example, every house in a village fenced, where, two months previously, none had been. Every individual feels that he has made a reasonable decision, but that he has made it as an individual.

THE ORGANIZATION OF LABOUR

The husband-wife team is the cultivating unit, except for single person households. Assistance even from adolescent children is rare. A man placed in great difficulty by an allergy of his wife, which made it impossible for her to work in mud, and who had a marriageable son and daughter in his house, still struggled along on his own. Modesty forbids nubile girls to work in the fields, and youths go off about their affairs with the peer-group, paying little attention to the routine organization of the parental household.

There are two ways of mobilizing a larger group. One is called *tolong-menolong* (helping out) and the other *menyeraya*.[1] The distinction between these two forms which informants stressed was that in the second the person aided is obliged to feed the workers, while in the first he is not. They also said that cooperative work was once more common than it is now, and that where *menyeraya* was once to be expected *tolong-menolong* is now more likely.

Tolong menolong is an expression of friendship, helping someone who is in trouble. A man whose wife is sick is the usual person to benefit from this help. It is not even necessary for him to ask for it. His neighbours, knowing that he is in trouble and behindhand with his work, agree amongst themselves to help him, inviting such other relatives and friends as they feel appropriate. They tell the man they are going to help him, and on the appointed morning go to the ricefield with their tools, and usually complete the work in one day.

Menyeraya must be organized according to *adat* rules. The person needing help, since he has to feed the workers, must also initiate the venture and invite the participants. Kin must be invited as if to a ceremonial, and the implications of not attending are the same as with a feast. *Menyeraya* was once a privilege of chiefs, magicians and midwives, although not confined to them. I have heard of

---

[1] *Menyeraya*. For this Wilkinson (1912) gives *seraya* to help, but Ahmad (1956) gives *suroh*, order. Both notions are present in the Jelebu use of the word.

chiefs elsewhere in the district occasionally having their fields cultivated in this way, but it is certainly not normal practice nowadays. The position of midwife was once a *pusaka* passing in one female line in a village. The midwife's knowledge obliged her to help anyone in the village requiring her services regardless of payment, and this, due to the taboos associated with child birth, was an onerous duty. The magician too was seen as someone helping the village, providing help to the sick and others as a duty, whether it was personally convenient or not. Nowadays the midwife and magician expect payment for their services beyond the traditional *adat*. In the past *menyeraya* was reciprocity for services rendered throughout the year; now that payment is given no obligation is created. That summarizes the general situation. But a magician who is prepared to be on call at all hours of the night, regardless of the weather, and who does not demand payment 'unless you care to give a little', can expect a good response if he is in trouble himself. The village magician's wife was seriously ill, but he did not *menyeraya*. Even so, every family in the village was represented at the *tolong-menolong* in his field, and many of his neighbours mentioned their obligation to the *dukun*, and his traditional right to *menyeraya*, in talking about it.

These forms of cooperation are used for preparing the fields but not for harvesting; for the latter labour will be hired if required. Labour is never hired to prepare the fields. For those in recognized need there are the institutions of *menyeraya* and *tolong-menolong*; others will rent out a field rather than hire workers. Payment of workers would leave little if any profit over the rent which can be received, and workers if hired would want payment at once, months before the crop was harvested.

For harvesting labour is frequently hired because of the need for speed. As the harvesters produce their own reward payment is not a problem. A large cultivator, faced with all his crop ripening at once, will find it worthwhile to hire labour. This labour is always paid in rice and the 'fixed' rate is 1/10th of the grain harvested by the worker. Calculation is made easy by the use of the traditional harvesting method. But if a man is known to be in great need he will not be able to get labour at that price. 'If he offers one they will want two, if two then three, if three then four, they'll even offer to split the crop with him.' There are, however, also people who want rice and welcome an opportunity to increase their supplies. A man known to be a surplus producer will be approached by these people and asked whether he needs help. The wife of a wealthy man is likely to be approached by her kin; they are sorry to see her with so much work to do, and offer their assistance (paid of course). Non-kin are franker, and admit that they would like more rice. In such cases the rate will keep to the fixed level.

Rich men even employ relatives and dependent families[1] as a form of charity. Their work is lessened, and the crop is got safely into storage more quickly, but the notion of helping the needy is also a factor in their decision to hire labour.

Even more people are willing to help harvest *pulut* than are ordinary rice. Every family needs some *pulut*, but not a great deal, unless a feast is being planned, and they often do not plant any.

Another method of mobilizing a larger group once common was that a number of men would agree to work on each other's land for one day at a time in rotation. Working together was quicker and more enjoyable. Villagers offered a number of reasons for abandoning the practice, 'I used to work with X, Y and Z until Z died.' Or 'we broke up because some people had cattle and some did not'. Or 'because so many people have gone away to work'. The groups were in any case small, of four or five men. When women cooperate, as they still sometimes do for planting, they do so with their kin. The cooperative work group of men is still occasionally tried, but there is no well-established group working from year to year. All work can normally be managed by the husband-wife team. Large work groups would also require that men devote themselves exclusively to rice cultivation during the period of the operation of the group, and this many men cannot do because of their dependence on regular rubber tapping.

FAILURE TO CULTIVATE

Sometimes a whole village does not cultivate for a year or more. A well-known case in Negri Sembilan is the Pantai area near Seremban. Pantai was famous for the splendid and beautiful houses of the Malay villagers. These were commonly explained by the wealth the people derived from the early introduction of rubber there. The fields were watered by a Government constructed dam and irrigation system. Never the less, year after year work

[1] See below p. 152.

in the fields was patchy at best, with areas left uncultivated, and hardly any coordination of activity. Discussion with Pantai people, and comments of Jelebu people on the situation, suggest that two factors were important. First of all Pantai shows an advanced stage in the trend to specialization in rubber production which may be seen even in Jelebu. Secondly, there was a change in the moral status of rice growing whereby it lost its special significance and valuation.

Where traditional culture experiences a shock it shows little resilience. In Pantai the disrupting factor was resettlement. Both Chinese and Malays were affected, all being moved into Pantai New Village, while the beautiful homes of the Malays decayed and their homesteads were overgrown. This affected their 'hearts'; work in the ricefields no longer seemed a worthwhile activity.

Neglect of rice cultivation can also be found in Jelebu. Here the villagers blame water, and say that if the Government would build them a dam they would cultivate. Water is certainly a problem, but neighbouring villages attribute this neglect of the ricefields to 'rubber-madness'. Objective changes in economic conditions have made rice cultivation less important. Although it is not an uneconomic activity the possibility of buying rice makes rice growing more a matter of choice than it would have been before the introduction of rubber. But rice retains a special value which disposes villagers to grow their own supplies even when they might buy. Anything which undermines this special status of rice cultivation is liable to give rise to cultivation problems of the type discussed here.

The shortage of water is also a value problem to some extent. The water was always there before. If they wished, the villagers could still construct dams with their traditional methods. The difficulty arises in organizing cooperation for collective work, together with the fact that the villagers can buy rice with their income from rubber.

Traditional leadership is no longer active, and no longer accepted as legitimate by all villagers. The only authority with anything approaching general acceptance is that of the new educated class, and such leadership is not available in the ricefield. Leadership in the village now depends to a very great extent on personality. If a leader is forceful, and prepared to work hard himself, cooperation of a simple kind can be organized. If there is no such personality the routine authority attached to an office such as that of *adat* chief or Government appointed *ketua* will not suffice. This situation is common to all villages, but it is more serious where the value of rice cultivation itself is questioned. It is significant that the two villages which had the most 'difficulties' with rice cultivation had been disturbed, in one case by the proximity of the District Capital and urban influences, in the other by involvement with the Communists and resettlement.

RICE SALES

Each year the Government announces the minimum price of rice. The villagers wish to receive this price. But the Government does not make arrangements to buy the rice at the fixed price should there be no private buyer willing to do so. In this area the problem is accentuated for the few surplus producers by the small quantity available, and that of a variety not liked by millers.

There is thus no certainty until some time after the harvest who will be buying the rice and at what price. Eventually complaints from the peasantry force the Government to find some buyer or to buy the rice itself. In 1959 and 1960 a group of peasants undertook the sale of grain themselves, buying it from other peasants at a price 50 c. less than the official price to cover the cost of lorry transport to Kuala Lumpur. Certainty of sale for their own crops was the main motive for this venture. 'After we have paid for the lorry, if we have to stay in Kuala Lumpur overnight there is no profit.'

There are also sales within the village. If the outside buyer is late in arriving villagers needing money try to find someone to buy their grain in the village. Wage-earners often do this, for they too feel more secure with a year's supply of rice in the house.

Under the Emergency Regulations the sale of rice was forbidden, indeed there were rules declaring the maximum which a man might store in his house. These regulations were a dead letter in the village where I lived, but even so people did not wish to publicize what they were doing, and so I have no reliable estimate of the total volume of village sales.

CHAPTER V

The Major Products: Rubber and Fruit

RUBBER

Rubber is a cash crop. Apart from occasional trivial use as glue for envelopes, or repairing punctured bicycle tyres, there is no direct use to which rubber can be put in the village.

Some people own enough rubber to afford to pay others to work it, others have just enough to work themselves; others again have none, and are obliged to share-tap to make a living.

Of 35 households in one village 16 did not own any rubber. Of the heads of these 16 households 3 had employment at least as profitable as rubber tapping, and one was a magician (*dukun*). The *dukun* was flourishing during the two years I was there, though he was later reduced to share-tapping. Unmarried sons are not included in this calculation, for to do so would greatly raise the proportion of tappers to owners. Most youths only enter the regular work force when they marry and acquire responsibilities. The figure 35 also includes some *janda* who did not tap, and old people who had disposed of their rubber.

As a generalization it may be said that most middle-aged men own some rubber. Nearly all old men have also owned rubber, but may have sold it or passed it on to their children. Land ownership amongst the young is much rarer, and is usually only found when a parent's death has led to early inheritance.

One reason for this age distribution of land ownership is the Government's land alienation policy since the introduction of the Stevenson scheme in 1922 (Bauer 1947, 1957). With minor exceptions no new land has been alienated since that date. Therefore the owners of land are those who were able to take advantage of the brief period between the introduction of the crop (dated by villagers at 1916 for Jelebu) and the restriction scheme, to acquire holdings.

Holdings are small, a reflection of the way in which planting was carried out. The villagers relied almost entirely on their own labour, so that only a small cash outlay was required. The acreage which an individual could undertake was therefore limited. The normal holding is of between two and four acres, and the man who owns more than the usual acreage more often holds it in two or three plots than in one large one.

TABLE I.   Ownership of rubber

Acreage	Number of Households
0	16
0–2	8
3–5	7
6–10	2
11–20	2
	35

The number of entries in the 6–20 classes would be larger if holdings owned in the general area of the village by wealthy outsiders were included. These lands, when not cleared for replanting, are an important source of employment for share-tappers, but they do not affect the proportions in each ownership class in village society.

A peasant would sell rubber land only if in great need. Most peasants do not have the cash reserves to buy such holdings as are sold, and rubber land sales tend to mean the concentration of holdings in the hands of those few individuals, peasants and officials, who have a surplus income. Such purchase, since it represents a further addition to their saveable income, increases their ability to buy more land when the opportunity arises. Inheritance can serve as a check on this trend but it cannot reverse it.

YIELDS AND INCOME

Village rubber is old and of poor quality. Much of it is diseased and has suffered from bad tapping. The usual lot for a tapper to work is about two acres, but this is not a precise measure because the trees are unevenly planted, some being densely packed while others stand alone in a mass of scrub.

The normal tapper produces every tapping day two or three sheets of rubber, each weighing between $2\frac{1}{2}$ and 3 katties. Daily yield is thus between 5 and 9 katties and most people are nearer the minimum. If a man got less than 5 katties a day the owner would not be satisfied, and would replace him, while if a tapping lot would not yield 5 katties a day a tapper would not wish to work it. (1 katty = 1⅓ lb.)

The product is usually divided in the ratio of 6 to the owner and 4 to the tapper. A higher share might be given to the tapper when the owner lives some distance from his land, and must rely on the industry and honesty of the tapper to maintain his property. A distant or poor holding would require a larger share to secure a tapper.

The trees cannot be tapped every day of the month. If they are tapped too frequently the latex flow lessens. Rain also restricts production. When the trunk of a tree is wet the latex spreads all over the trunk, instead of flowing down to the cup in channels cut in the bark. The villagers also say that tapping when the tree is wet causes mouldy rot. I inquired why Chinese were prepared to tap on days which the Malay said were too wet. 'Because they do not care what happens to the trees.'

On Malay holdings there is dense undergrowth around the trees, so that they take some time to dry after rain; hence small-holders lose more days tapping because of rain than do estates. Moreover, since working in the wet scrub is cold and unpleasant, a tapper who has worked for several days will take a holiday after a rainy night. If, however, a number of days have been lost in quick succession, his need of money will make the tapper brave a slightly wet day.

A long dry spell permits tapping every day, but lessens the latex yield, so that the tapper may decide not to tap, but to save the bark of the tree.

Twenty tapping days a month is regarded as a reasonable work-ing month. After about a week's uninterrupted tapping the worker will stop for a day or two of his own accord, but if rain is falling every few days the worker will not take voluntary holidays, but will follow the dictates of the weather.

The competition of other forms of work may attract a man from rubber tapping. It is not always possible for a tapper to continue work right through the rice cultivation season and at harvest time, although he will try to do so. The fruit harvest is another strong competitor. Even men who have no fruit of their own have the chance to earn more money for pleasanter work, plucking and carrying fruit for others.

Feasts and ceremonies also lead to some loss of tapping time. But modern feasts have had to be curtailed in the interests of tapping work. Feasts are shorter; only those men most directly concerned will stop work for a feast, and all cooperative work, such as preparing cooking places and awnings, has to be done during the afternoon, when tappers are free.

Muslims are obliged to celebrate the two *hari raya*, one after the fasting month and the other at the end of the *Haj* pilgrimage. And especially after a month's fasting there is great willingness to celebrate. For this day, and the days immediately following, all work is at a standstill as people visit and receive visits from their kin and friends. If the feast falls at a prosperous time, say after the rice or fruit harvest, people are most reluctant to resume the routine of daily tapping, while owners whose holdings are yielding no income complain about the Malay as a worker compared with the Chinese. But should *hari raya* fall at a difficult time, two or three days later most of the people will have resumed tapping.

The average tapper, then, will earn two or three dollars a day for a twenty-day working month, giving him an income of between $40.00 and $60.00. He will probably not reach this figure in December which is the height of the rainy season. In 1954 the villagers lost eighteen consecutive days tapping through rain, as well as other odd days, and their hardship was worsened by having to buy rice, since it was impossible to sun-dry paddy before husking it.

Some owners, unable to tap themselves, are merely sharing the product of a holding, sufficient to occupy one worker, with the tapper. In this case they will have an income only a little more than the tappers. The owner-tapper is likely to have an income higher than either of the first two categories, but this may not be noticeable in a higher standard of living. The owner of a small holding who does not tap it himself probably does not have heavy economic responsibilities; frequently he is old and no longer supporting a family. The owner-tapper, on the other hand, is likely to be a man still bearing family responsibilities. Again, although the owner-tapper receives both shares he cannot choose where he will tap, while the share-tapper is free to seek a high quality holding, the higher yield from which will go some or all of the way to making up the difference in income compared with the owner-tapper.

I am not arguing that there is income equality between the three categories of small-owner, share-tapper, and owner-tapper, but merely that these are not clear income classes. It is the men with enough land to employ three or four share-tappers who form a consumption class above most of the villagers. These are the men who form the village upper class, and have a surplus which they can use for further accumulation of property. Ten to twenty acres make a man rich among Jelebu peasantry, a degree of income differentiation much less than is found elsewhere in Malay society; for example, an investigation in the Batu Pahat area of Johore found several peasants owning more than 100 acres (S. Hussin Ali, 1960).

The lack of differentiation in Jelebu I regard as normal, and feel that it is the greater differentiation which has to be explained. Their first holdings the peasants made with their own labour, a power approximately equal. Only when some men can mobilize greater labour power than their fellows will there be inequality from the start, with this initial inequality providing the basis for progressively increasing concentration of land ownership. In-dentured Javanese provided this labour supply in Johore. These *orang tebusan* were brought to Singapore by brokers who would pass on the right to their services to whoever redeemed them. In this way a wealthy man could secure control of labour as he could not, for example, in Negri Sembilan, and the greater income differentiation in Johore is one result of this form of servitude (S. Hussin Ali, 1960).

TECHNIQUES

Rubber production is simple. Early in the morning, when the sap flow is greatest, the tapper cuts a thin strip from the bark of the tree. The latex then flows down channels cut in the bark into a porcelain cup held in position by a 'spoon' driven into the trunk. Some three or four hours later this latex is collected. Next the rubber is coagulated, and rolled into sheets through two mangles. Dealers will pay slightly more for a thin sheet, especially if it has been coagulated and rolled with care. All work should be completed by noon, although a worker from a distant holding will take longer. Crowding of machines also wastes the workers' time.

The larger land-owners own their machines, which are used free by their tappers. People who do not own machines, or whose employers do not, pay $1.00 a month to use them. This money, as well as the cost of the coagulating acid, is paid by the owner, not the share-tapper.

The sheet should be dried for two or three days before it is sold. Newly rolled sheet sells at a lower price. The wetter sheet is heavier, but the villagers maintain that the lower price more than makes up for the greater weight, so it is unprofitable to sell too quickly. The difference is not great, and will not matter to the peasant who needs money badly after some days of rain, but the loss is appreciable on the output of several days' tapping. A higher price can be obtained for extra dry sheet. Here again the peasants assert that the increased price does not compensate for the loss in weight. The first point I believe, the second I was never able to test. Selling too soon is very common, but I never met a peasant storing rubber to the point where it might be called extra dry!

The rubber now passes out of Malay hands, and whatever increase in value it acquires after further processing is of no benefit to the villagers. A small smoke house is technically possible, and would be an economic proposition for a large owner, even if he only dried his own sheet. No villager does run a smokehouse, and even a cooperative smokehouse built with Government help in one of the larger Jelebu villages was forced to close.

The smokehouse flourished during the price depression after the Korean war when even a few cents difference in price seemed important. When the price rose again the peasants preferred to sell their unsmoked sheet to a dealer, and get their money as quickly as possible.

The holding itself requires some attention. Periodically the worst of the scrub around the trees must be cleared. The tapper will not do this unless paid by the owner. An owner employing tappers will usually pay someone to do it. The charge for clearing an acre may be as much as $30.00 but the price fixed varies with factors such as the length of time the holding has been left un-cleared and the need of the worker for money.

Some men specialize in odd jobs of this kind. They are usually young men raising large families. They are considered especially industrious, but the quality which owners stress is reliability. Many men will offer their services for clearing a holding, or repairing a roof, but only a few of them are regarded as reliable enough to do a good job, or even to do the job at all after they have received the initial payment. Poor relatives feel that if there is paid work to be done it should be given to them. The prospective employer is placed in a quandary; he knows that he should favour kin, but he cannot trust them to do a good job. A relative, if employed, is liable to trade on his relationship to do the minimum of work; if he is not employed he is resentful.

LABOUR

A man working his own holding has no organizational problems beyond the allocation of his own time. This, moreover, is largely determined by conventional ideas on what constitutes a reasonable day's work and a reasonable income, and by the technique of production. In the peasant rubber industry organizational problems are largely questions of the relations between owner and tapper, an issue that has already had brief mention.

There is a marked similarity to owner-tenant relations in rice cultivation. Only when there are kinship ties between the parties is there any durability in the relationship.

Owners complain continually of their tappers, but it is usually the tappers who stop work rather than the owner who sacks them. Although the owner of a lot known to be without a tapper will be approached by men seeking work they are nearly always men who already have lots which they want to leave, or who have voluntarily left their previous lot. Better trees or a more accessible lot were among the benefits sought from a change, but workers also move because they are tired of the continual complaints of their employer, or because they want a rest from tapping and 'stop', sure that they will be able to find another lot when they want to start work again.

Owners complain that the workers take too many holidays, decide it is too wet when other people are tapping, do not get enough rubber from the trees, are unskilful, wasting bark, cutting the trunk, or leaving too much scrap in the cups after collection. They complain that the coolies (workers) want to sell too soon, and are always trying to borrow the owner's share. Especially when the two big feasts are drawing near owners complain that the workers do not seem to realize that owners have to celebrate too.

These complaints, and the high labour turnover, are indications of a labour shortage. The rate for tappers' shares does not change, but tappers are able to demand loans from their employers. If the owner will not accommodate them they leave his employ, leaving outstanding debts unpaid, sure that they will find another lot. The owner realizes that he cannot avoid giving these loans if he wants to retain his labour, but he resents having to make a payment which was not part of the original bargain. The labourers' demands for loans, and the owners' attempts to avoid them, lead to tension and mutual resentment.

Labour is scarce because of the fixed shares of owner and tapper. A higher share for tappers would induce some owners to tap their own trees rather than employ others. Poor holdings would be allowed to remain untapped, and the higher income for tappers might even directly increase the labour supply by inducing young men working elsewhere to return to the village, or by dissuading young men from leaving. This I doubt, however, for young men leave the village simply to get away from it.

The Emergency served to reduce the available supply of tapping labour. It provided opportunities for labour outside the village for young men who would otherwise have been share-tappers. The Emergency also decreased the supply of Chinese labour for tapping, both through resettlement and through the widening of social distance between the races. Informants (owners) asserted that before the Emergency 'no one' used Malays as tappers. Chinese are regular, keep to the bargain and do not ask for loans or favours. They work to maximize their own income and therefore that of their employers. Because they are dependent on one source of income, and have fixed cash obligations, they do not take unnecessary holidays. This picture of the Chinese tapper is highly idealized, but it does show what the owner dislikes about Malay tappers.

There are still some Chinese tappers, and their work can be compared with that of Malays to show that there is some substance in the owners' complaints. But nowadays Chinese will not usually work for shares. They prefer the arrangement known as *pajak*, by which a holding is rented for a fixed sum, and the renter keeps whatever he can make out of it. This has attractions for Malay owners; whatever the weather or whatever happens to the price of rubber, the money comes in without argument or fuss.

The drawback is that the yield from the trees varies with tapping practice. Longer and more numerous cuts, taking more bark from the tree, will increase the yield for a while. But the tree may be killed, and the rate of bark consumption will certainly exceed the natural regrowth. So at the end of the agreement the owner may find that his source of income had been destroyed, or at least lost for a long period.

A Malay disposed of the tapping rights to 4 acres of poor rubber for $1.00 a day to a Chinese brother and sister. Within a few days of the Chinese starting the owner was unhappy and within a fortnight desperate, for the Chinese were getting 7 *sheets* of rubber a day, tapping right up into the branches with ladders, and tapping every day. They had paid in advance and were not willing to break the agreement. Eventually they were persuaded to do so by the *ketua kampong*, for Chinese having dealings in the villages must be careful of Malay opinion. The trees could not be tapped again for another two years, and then only sporadically, by men who quickly left for other holdings.

Tappers are not all equally skilful and careful. Bark consumption, damage to the trees, and yield, all depend on the tapper's skill and care. A bad tapper may be tolerated, but even if sacked he soon finds other employment. The quality of sheet varies too; some tappers, working for the same owner on neighbouring lots, using the same acid and machines, always produce sheet worth a few cents a katty less than that of their fellows. A difference of 2 or 3 cents a katty may irritate an owner, but would not lead him to replace the worker; however, there are examples where the difference is as much as 10 c. below the normal price, and even more below the bonus price which a good worker can obtain.

The scrap rubber left in the channels and cups after the latex has been collected belongs to the worker, and sells for about 30 c. per katty. As it does not have to be shared it is nearly as valuable to the worker as sheet rubber, especially as there is no chore of machining it and rubbish can be mixed in. The tapper, anxious to finish early, who collects the latex while it is still flowing, or who does not bother to visit all the trees he has tapped, will get more scrap than a good worker. Owners keep a jealous eye on their coolies' scrap.

Durable owner-tapper relations are all between relatives or

affines, and because of matrilocality, usually between affines. The tapper is able to regard the holding as to some extent his, and the owner to regard giving employment to a relative as a worthy act. The owner can also feel that he is helping the *tempat semanda*; through him the tapper's wife and children are receiving an income. Loans to the tapper too can be seen as part of this same obligation, and should kinship reasons keep the tapper from working the owner is also probably involved and hence will appreciate the importance of the matter, while an unrelated owner is more likely to be put out by his loss of income. The owner's wife's relations with her sisters are also very important; in one case well known to me the relations between owner and tapper (*biras*) were in perpetual crisis, but they could not break the relationship because their wives would not let them (or perhaps the good relations of wives left the *biras* free to express their ambivalence without fear of total rupture). Finally, by employing a relative the owner can feel surer that he will not meet the extremes of malevolence and dishonesty some tappers direct against their employers.

Despite the fact that these relationships persist, and hence presumably bring a net advantage, there is much ambivalence, and both parties also wish for a relationship unencumbered with kinship. The owner resents his lack of freedom to change the worker, and the worker resents his inferiority and dependence on someone he meets as equal in kinship contexts.

SALES

All the important dealers are Chinese. They form a price-ring in the local town, adjusting their prices to the latest Singapore quotations, but not competing through price amongst themselves.

Some of the wealthier peasants have friendly ties with a dealer and always sell their rubber through him. This is advantageous to the dealer who cannot offer price incentives. What he can offer are other small benefits. The friendship allows the peasant to feel that he will be given a fair deal at all times without having to be continually on his guard. When shopping he will use the dealer's shop as a place to leave his bicycle and purchases. If short of money he can always borrow a few dollars from the dealer. Some of these ties date back to the previous generation, but in the past the ties were closer. Before the creation of Malay Reservations some of the Chinese had interests in the development of Malay holdings, and some owned land in the area. When no longer permitted to own land some of them operated for a while through Malay 'straw men', choosing not poor villagers who would allow their names to be used for a few dollars, but wealthy Malays whom they could trust. This type of tie no longer exists, but friendships dating to that period still affect economic relationships. Because of the Government's economic policy Malays are favoured in the allocation of licences, and so may be able to get licences to operate as rubber dealers when Chinese cannot. There are, therefore, a few cases where dealers are operating under Malay names, but even here there is always substantial Chinese participation in the venture, even if the licence holder is not actually allowing others to use his licence for a payment.

The price paid for rubber in Jelebu follows closely that paid in Singapore. Allowing for variations in quality, the price the villagers receive is about 10 c. per katty ($1\frac{1}{3}$ lb.) less than the price per pound No. 1 R.S.S. in Singapore. This is not a precise measure of the margin between the prices because peasant rubber, however good it may be by village standards, is never better than second grade by international market standards, and is unsmoked.

FRUIT: DURIAN AND LANGSAT

The two main varieties of fruit in Jelebu are the *langsat* and the *durian*. Large quantities of pineapple and banana are also grown but these enterprises are mainly Chinese, although carried out on Malay land. Other local fruits, such as mangosteens and jack fruit, are grown, but do not give rise to a large commerce. Some peasants have recently planted a superior variety of *rambutan*, which has become popular in Malaya, and many more are talking about doing so, but this fruit is not yet available in any quantity in Jelebu.

Until there were urban markets, and modern transport to get the fruit to market, there was no commercial demand for the fruit crop. Traditionally there were no exclusive rights to fruit orchards, as opposed to fruit trees on homestead land. Extended families had a superior claim to collect fruit at certain places in the jungle, but this was not exclusive, and there were no individual rights within the group. Private land ownership was introduced by the British. Among fruit holdings now individually owned by Malays are some which formerly belonged to the aborigines, for these were the places where they gathered to eat fruit, and by dispersing the seeds, increased the number of trees. Fruit land is not usually legal *pusaka*, for it was not individually held when titles were first registered.

Malay orchards (*dusun*) are largely patches of self-sown trees in the jungle. Fruit trees are also found on homesteads, but these are not a major source of supply. The bulk of the fruit comes from the jungle holdings. Owners confine their attentions to clearing around trees before harvest, and perhaps also clearing a little around fruit seedlings to aid their growth.

It follows that acreages of *dusun* are even less significant than figures of village rubber acreages as an indication of output capacity. A rubber holding at least will be largely rubber, but an acre of *dusun* may contain very few fruit trees. Another complication is the great irregularity of yield which characterizes both important local fruits. If there is any regular cycle of fruiting the villagers do not know it, and it is certainly not an annual one. The harvests, when they come, vary greatly in quantity, both from harvest to harvest and between neighbouring areas at the same harvest.

The economic significance of the harvest depends on the income realized rather than the physical quantity. Prices fluctuate greatly. They are determined in the State capital, to which most fruit is taken, to be sold either retail there or sent to other towns. Price variations in the town may well not reflect conditions in one small valley. A small crop from one valley may not get scarcity prices if there are abundant supplies from other sources; on the other hand, a large harvest may get bumper prices, if no-one else is selling fruit. These happy conditions were realized in 1950, and ten years later the villagers still referred to that time when they spoke of a good year for fruit.

At the harvests I have seen the first fruit received good prices, $8.50 a box for *langsat* and 80 c. a fruit for *durian*, but prices begin to fall rapidly, dropping a dollar or 50 c. for *langsat* daily until they reach about $3.00 for *langsat* and 40 c. for *durian*. Informants could recall gluts in which the price of *langsat* dropped as low as $1.50 a box, but it has not done so for some years, and there is an important rigidity, the cost of labour, which tends to maintain the price about the $3.00 level.

The ownership pattern for fruit land is similar to that for rubber, save that more people own some. Poorer villagers may have only a few trees on their house sites, while a wealthy man may own ten acres or more. There is also a tendency to concentration. A poor peasant seeking cash would relinquish possession of *dusun* more readily than he would rice or rubber land, for it can make only an irregular contribution to his consumption. It is, however, an attractive enough investment for the wealthy villager seeking to accumulate property should there be no rubber land competing for his savings at the same time.

A large owner of fruit may hope to receive $1,000 or more from a reasonably good crop; even the poor man with only a few trees can hope to get $50 to $100.00. This income is irregular, and cannot be relied upon for regular consumption expenses. But rice and rubber are for that. Fruit provides an uncommitted lump sum for purposes which cannot be managed out of regular income. This is the quality which makes it so important to the village economy.

THE SALE OF FRUIT

Fruit is sold to Chinese dealers who collect from fixed points at the roadside every day of the season. An occasional Malay will try to take the fruit to the State Capital on his own, hiring a car or taking the fruit by bus, but he never perseveres. The greatest disadvantage he faces is lack of knowledge of the fruit market and of contacts in town. He cannot know what the price of fruit will be when he reaches the market, and he does not have permanent relations with any one market dealer to protect him from a disastrous fall in prices. Above all, he does not have the capital, and access to fruit supplies, which alone would enable him to operate on a large enough scale to make a worthwhile profit.

The Malay appears as a buying agent for the Chinese. Dealers are competing for supplies of fruit, but not through prices. A dealer might offer an extra 10 c. a box 'on the quiet' to a large supplier, but the dealers are regulated in their competition by their notions of normal profit, and their desire to avoid cut-throat competition (there are only four main purchasers for the area). Competition takes the form of trying to strike exclusive bargains with Malay collecting agents, or with large owners. The dealer can only offer the same terms as his competitors, to take as many boxes of fruit as the supplier can provide at such and such a price (subject to alteration as the market changes, but not without warning); the Malay chooses between the dealers on personal grounds. A long acquaintance, or friendly treatment in the past (and these dealers have much business with the villagers), may incline him towards one dealer, some slight may turn him against another. Reliability is the important quality.

Collectors are either regular or occasional. Many of the first type are village shopkeepers, who, with their site at the roadside and having to spend the whole day there, are well placed for the work. In places far from a shop a villager known to the Chinese, and regarded as trustworthy, undertakes the work. The importance of knowledge and trust cannot be over stressed. A Malay may have helped a Chinese during the Japanese terror, thus creating a life-long tie. Or the Chinese may have had a vegetable garden on land behind a Malay village and struck up a friendship with a Malay who helped him in his relations with the other villagers. There is not sufficient moral community between Malays and Chinese for them to have prolonged economic relations requiring trust without some such particularistic tie of this kind. I was struck by the way the Chinese is regarded as fair game; cheating and theft from a Chinese are rather a joke. But it must also be admitted that the Chinese organize their economic affairs along particularistic lines even within their own ethnic group where sanctions can be much more readily applied.

The regular collector is supplied with boxes for *langsat*, and also with a cash advance if the volume of business warrants it. 50 c. a box is the usual collector's commission, and this will give a successful collector an income of between $10.00 and $15.00 a day while the season is at its height. Some collectors try to increase their income by cutting the price they give the growers. Such a policy will lead to the failure, or at least great reduction, of their business, as growers quickly turn to another collector.

Durian are sold by the fruit, and this makes collecting a more complex business. The 'fruit' is a notional one; only rarely is an actual *durian* equal to a 'fruit'. The collector bargains with the grower as to whether two, three or even four fruit are equal to one 'fruit'. Then he rearranges them so that those he sells the dealer amount to more than he bought from the grower. Apart from this he receives commission from the dealer. An experienced collector whose affairs I studied expected to receive between $5.00 and $6.00 per day from commission, and another $4.00 or $5.00 from rearranging the fruit. Another way in which the collector can make money is greatly resented by the dealer. He can select the really good fruit and sell them to another dealer at a premium price. His regular dealer will not pay more, for he is expected to take all the inferior fruit along with the good ones. Suspicion of this practice will soon end the relationship between dealer and collector.

Many villagers are prepared to try for the easy earnings of fruit dealing. They are not sought by the dealer, nor given boxes or advances. They seek him out, inquiring prices and times of collection. The occasional collector seeks to make a profit from the sale of his own fruit, that of his kin, and that of neighbours whose crop is too small for them to want to bother to take it to the shop to sell. The small scale collectors operate with little capital, and where possible delay payment until they in turn have been paid for the fruit. Most of them are quickly discouraged by the small returns, and many of them ruin their chances by trying to cut the price they promised in the morning when they see how small their return for the day will be, or when they have been offered less than they had anticipated by the dealer. All large owners prefer the uncomplicated transaction with a regular collector, if indeed they do not go straight to the Chinese, to the personal and uncertain relations with the occasional collector, and without access to these large sources of supply he cannot prosper.

Fruit is sometimes sold on the tree before it is ripe. This sale is known as *pajak* (as with renting out a rubber holding). The price paid is always much lower than the eventual selling price 'should' be, but has some attraction as an immediate and certain return, avoiding the risks of price fluctuations and damage from squirrels, flying foxes, rainstorms etc. Most villagers regard *pajak* as a loss, and will only *pajak* when unable to handle the fruit themselves. Wage-earners owning property in the village are almost forced to have their fruit handled in this way. Even the local owner, if he lives some distance from his holding, may lose much of it through theft, which he can avoid if he *pajak* with someone living nearby. Chinese are prepared to *pajak* fruit if there is some quantity, and may also hire a villager to guard it: people have been known to pluck and sell fruit which had already been sold.

An absent owner, or an old woman owner, can also arrange to divide the crop with someone. The usual bargain is two shares to the owner and one to the worker who watches and handles the fruit, but for a poor crop equal shares would be demanded. This arrangement is especially preferred for *durian* where the fruit are not plucked but collected as they fall. When the fruit are ripe and falling continuously the villagers construct lean-tos in the orchards and spend the night there, for the thud of *durian* falling may attract thieves. Dividing the crop gives a higher return than *pajak* but the owner runs the risk of being cheated.

Langsat have to be plucked. Owners of a few trees do this themselves. Should they be unable to do so, or should there be much fruit, labour must be hired. The standard rate is $1.00 a box for plucking and 50 c. for carrying it to the roadside. This price does not vary with the price of fruit, and this limits, I think, the price to which fruit could fall, especially as the carrying charge is greater for more remote villages.

The work payments spread the benefit of the crop to people who do not have fruit themselves. The same men are chosen for this work as for odd jobs, those known as reliable; a careless harvester damages the fruit by shaking it down, and loses the unripe fruit which should be left on the tree. Also, a man who has had the rewarding task of harvesting the bulk of the crop should be prepared to go back and collect the remainder at a later date. This obligation cannot be enforced, however, hence the stress on choosing trustworthy men.

When the harvest is good nearly everyone who wants work can get it, receiving an income many times what might be earned share-tapping for pleasanter work. The rubber owner, especially if he has no trees in fruit, has good cause for complaint, as his tappers stop work to harvest fruit or to try their luck as occasional collectors.

OTHER ECONOMIC ACTIVITIES

Compared with the production of the three crops discussed above, all other village economic activities are minor, either because of the small value of output, or because carried on by so few people.

THATCHMAKING

Sago leaf thatch is the traditional roofing material; even the Chinese, who use tiles for their town houses, use thatch for other buildings. Despite increasing competition from metal roofing extensive use is still made of thatch. A Malay villager may make his own, but all that used by Chinese is bought from Malays through the village shopkeeper.

Thatchmaking is the speciality of only a few villagers, although any of them may make it at one time or another. Old men, share-tappers anxious to increase their incomes (and even their wives), and some women who lack other support, are the regular thatch makers.

Sago trees are found dotted about the village, but the major sources of leaves for the regular makers are patches of trees planted on swampy soil. The village I studied had two of these, one of half, the other of about a quarter acre. The owners were wealthy and did not undertake thatchmaking themselves. Instead they allowed others to use the leaves in return for one half of the sheets of thatching made. In addition the maker has to supply his own bamboo and rattan.

The usual price per sheet is between 13 c. and 15 c., and the shopkeeper sells at 17 c. or 18 c. At such a price only the needy are interested in thatchmaking, except when the weather is poor and there is a general shortage of money. To make ten sheets would be regarded as a good day's work. Of this the maker, if sharing, will get only five sheets; hence he can expect to receive 65 c.

With thatch intended for sale at the shop the leaves are thinly placed and poorly sewn, but for village sale such work would not be acceptable. A villager needing thatch orders it from one of the acknowledged experts, usually an old man, and pays more than the price offered at the shop. Convenience and prestige favour metal roofs, and all the houses made while I was in the village had them, but there is still a regular market selling thatch to the Chinese who place their orders with the village shopkeeper.

CATTLE REARING

Most men rear one or two head of cattle. A rich man might own as many as ten, but this would be an unusually large herd; even the rich do not normally own more than five or six.

Malay cattle are not milked; their yield is their increase in value with growth, their calves, and with grown trained bulls, their use in rice growing.

Grazing, and the need for supervision and care, limit the

number of cattle owned. For about four months every year, when the ricefields are fallow, there is enough pasture, but as the rice season proceeds the grazing becomes increasingly scarce. Cattle are either tethered during the day and allowed to graze under supervision for a while in the evening, or they are taken to the jungle. This involves driving them to and fro, and guarding them during the day. An old man does this himself, but other owners, unless they have a young son free, have to pay a lad at least 50 c. a day to do it. Also, as previously mentioned, owners are often reduced to collecting grass to supplement grazing.

Cattle also require other care. Stalls have to be built and maintained, the cattle stalled every night, fires lit to keep away mosquitoes. Also cattle become sick, get lost, are attacked by tigers, or through straying they become the occasion of village quarrels. Such worries make owning a large herd a major problem.

Finally, cattle are not a very profitable investment. A good beast will be worth at least $200.00. If a man has five grown cattle they represent $1,000 and this can be turned into a desirable land investment, for an acre of village rubber will sell for between $200.00 and $500.00 and an acre of *dusun* for between $100.00 and $200.00.

One way to manage a large herd is to give some of them to someone to rear, sharing the issue equally with him. Poor men like this arrangement since it enables them to acquire some property, but the rich man does not want to hold a lot of his property in this way. For most villagers to allow others to care for their cattle is rather a charitable act than a purely economic transaction. Young men working outside the village may save in this way. They have an appreciating asset, and at the same time are helping the kinsman or affine who cares for it. Sheep or goats, of which most families have a few head, may be shared in the same way, but this practice is almost entirely confined to people living outside the village.

The place of cattle in the village economy cannot be understood unless it is realized that owning cattle is a favoured way of holding reserves (Swift, 1957).

CHICKEN RAISING

Every house has a few chickens, fed a little paddy and kitchen scraps, but relying mainly on foraging about the homestead.

The chicken is regarded as a valuable standby. If money is needed a grown chicken is always worth two dollars, and should un-unexpected guests arrive a chicken will provide a small feast.

Raising chickens is woman's work, and any money she can make from it should be hers. In a poor household there is usually too little money for this rule to be followed; a chicken is sold when money is needed and the question of whose money it is hardly arises. But domestic discord will soon result if a husband starts selling chickens simply because he is too lazy to tap. Two divorces followed from this cause in my village, although in each case it was revoked (*rojok*) within a few days. Richer peasants follow the rule, and may indeed make a show of knowing nothing about chickens, a matter for their wives.

SHOPKEEPING

Shopkeeping has always attracted villagers. Informants can relate that X used to have a shop here and Y a shop there. All agree how-ever that before the Emergency the Chinese were the biggest and most successful village shopkeepers. The Chinese, they say, kept a big stock, sold cheaply, and did not make a lot of fuss about a few small debts, as Malays do.

The Emergency removed Chinese competition, and there are now successful Malay enterprises, which have persisted for some years, and can support the owner and his family.

The shops stock mainly non-perishables in constant daily use. Spices, onions, oil, paraffin and matches, sugar, tea and coffee, soap, needles and thread, biscuits, potatoes, and perhaps a few Hong-Kong T-shirts. Combined with the provision store is a coffee-shop selling tea, coffee and soft drinks, perhaps Malay cakes made by the owner's wife or other village women, or bread and buns delivered by the Chinese bakery man.

The shop sells things that people forgot to buy in town, or it sells to old people and unmarried women who do not regularly go to town. The shopkeeper purchases most of his stock retail for the same price as any other villager. He then resells in the village at a higher price. Only with locally made coffee powders, tea dust and biscuits can he get a wholesale price, buying from the agents who pass his roadside shop on their way to visit the town shops. This is an important source of stocks only available to well-established village shops. $500.00 would be a generous estimate of the capital involved in a village shop, excluding the premises.

The village shop also buys from the villagers. The collection of fruit and thatch have already been mentioned. The shopkeeper may also deal in scrap rubber, buying for less than the town price from tappers who have no owner's licence, and hence cannot sell their own, or he may buy rice after the harvest from people who want ready money quickly.

These shops operate on a high profit margin and a small turn-over. They cannot change to the more profitable combination of high turnover and low margins because they have neither capital nor access to credit. High prices, and stale and unvaried stocks, place the shopkeeper at a disadvantage with his town competitor. During my stay this disadvantage was increased by the restrictions on types of goods which might be kept under the Emergency Regulations.

Town shops can easily get credit from wholesalers. This is partly a matter of business; the village shopkeeper can be neither an important customer nor a good credit risk. But I think there is also an ethnic factor involved. Pre-war Chinese shopkeepers in the village could obtain credit. It is noteworthy that the two most successful shopkeepers in the *mukim* speak some Chinese and are known as 'used to' (*biasa*) them. I think the ability to speak Chinese disposes the Chinese to regard these men favourably in a largely extra-rational way, for the wholesalers' agents speak Malay, and normally do so even with these Chinese-speaking Malays.

Credit for customers is a great problem for the shopkeeper. Villagers are angry if refused credit. But with their small incomes there is a great temptation to use money when received for further consumption (at another shop) rather than to pay debts. If the shopkeeper controlled the sale of their produce he would have some means of securing repayment, but this is only possible with the thatchmakers and even they can go elsewhere with their thatch. Should the shopkeeper allow debts to accumulate, wait patiently for his money if he sees the debtor resume cash purchases, or should he demand repayment? If he does not, the chances are that he will never get his money back; if he does, it is likely that the debtor will be extremely angry, and will not pay his debts or deal there again or recognize any of the ties which bind kin and neighbours together.

The villagers see the shopkeeper as a kinsman or neighbour, obliged to help them with small gifts or loans of consumption goods. And he has an abundance of goods. Even the Chinese was never as mean as our relative! If the Chinese were in fact more lenient there are two possible reasons for this. First of all they had to be. Quarrelling with one villager could easily turn the whole village against a shopkeeper, for he is a foreigner. Secondly, with a bigger business and more capital and credit they could afford to be. The Malay cannot allow his meagre capital to be tied up in debts, even if these debts will eventually be paid. I know of shops which have failed with two or three hundred dollars worth of debts outstanding.

Perhaps the Chinese merely seemed more lenient since the villagers judged their behaviour by different standards. No-one gets angry if a Chinese shopkeeper in town tries to recover his debts; indeed many people seem to treat the situation as a battle of wits, trying to avoid meeting him, or to calm him with a portion of the debt while avoiding full payment.

CHAPTER VI

Saving and Capital

I have discussed elsewhere (Swift, 1957 & 1963) the methods and sources of savings in this economy, and the role and form of capital in production. With regard to saving the main points were the emphasis on jewels, cattle and tangibles generally, and the importance of fruit income, rather than regular receipts from rubber, as the major source of savings.

With regard to capital I stress a distinction between fixed and working capital. The former, largely developed land, has, under the present circumstances, the nature of a fixed stock, especially where the very important asset rubber land is concerned, because of the Government refusal to alienate land for rubber planting, and the peasants' own reluctance to replant old or damaged holdings. The important characteristic of all three forms of production, where working capital is concerned, is the limited quantities which must be combined with labour and the fixed assets to produce an income.

The regular receipt of rubber income, the small need for working capital, and the way in which fruit income can be used to finance 'extraordinary expenditures' remove the three major causes of indebtedness among peasantry. Indebtedness is further lessened by the fact that the area is Malay Reservation and so could be loan security only for Malays, who do not practise usury. Also, ceremonial expenditures are smaller than elsewhere in Malaya, so there are not the same social pressures to borrow for ceremonial display.

Although credit does not play an important part in the organization of the village economy, loans have some significance in the social relations between individuals, and I shall discuss them here because of the insight they give into Malay economic attitudes.

Not to give a loan to a fellow villager is mean, and even to insist on repayment is not well regarded. A loan may be needed suddenly, perhaps to pay quit-rent, or to buy goods if unexpected guests arrive. Liability for quit-rent is known well in advance. The sums are, moreover, small, $2.00 or $4.00 per acre, depending on the type of land. Even so, many of the peasants are caught unprepared when they receive a notice threatening the auction of their land for non-payment of quit rent. A moderately well-to-do man can pay out of current income, but a share-tapper, with tax to pay on homestead, rice land or orchard, may well not have the money at once, and the aged or *janda* are in an even more serious position. So they are forced to borrow. Or a man may need money to visit a sick relative. Or people hire village craftsmen and promise payment when they harvest their rice.

The harvest is the traditional time for the payment of debts, and when these are paid in rice they are usually calculated by a traditional fixed value of rice—one bushel equals 50 cents.

The villager knows, when he makes a small loan, that he is liable not to be repaid, or at least, not without unpleasantness that can seriously affect his social ties. Therefore people tend to regard small loans as a form of charity, and not to lend more than they would be prepared to lose.

Occasionally a villager has need of a greater sum. No one but very close relatives would be willing to make a large loan without security, and they may not be able to do so. The security most usually offered for large loans is fruit land, which passes to the lender, with all it yields, until such time as the loan is repaid. If the borrower repays promptly the lender may get no return at all, but if payment is delayed the return may be many times greater than the principal. One man pledged his *durian* orchard for $100.00 six years ago. The trees have borne fruit four times but the creditor refuses to return the orchard until the loan is repaid. This temporary sale (known as *pajak*) is regarded as giving security rather than a return on the loan. The latter would seem too like usury.

There is a form of loan association known as *kutu*. Here a number of men, usually between five and ten, pay a sum fortnightly or monthly into a pool which is taken by one of them in turn until all have received a share, when the *kutu* dissolves. In wage-earning groups, such as the Chinese and the Indian dock labourers of Singapore, such *kutu* have great durability, but among Jelebu Malays they are formed only occasionally, and rarely function smoothly until everyone has received his share.

It is difficult to get together enough members to make a *kutu* worthwhile. A man in need of a fairly large amount of cash may find that he can get two or three friends to join him, but this will only give a small amount at each division. To collect more members requires great persuasion, and often moral bullying. The organizer will maintain that anyone who refuses to join either does not want to help him or does not trust him, is a miser in fact. The reluctant lender protests that this is not the case, but to prove it feels obliged to join the *kutu*.This type of pressure is particularly effective on young unmarried tappers, who do not, after all, really need all the money they earn.

People say they do not like to join *kutu* because they do not trust those who draw early to keep up their payments, and they doubt their own ability to maintain a regular payment for several weeks. These expectations are often fulfilled. If one member is unable to pay, even for respectable reasons, the scheme will collapse, for the others will not be willing to go on risking their money.

There is also some deliberate cheating. In one case the third sharer took his money and went to Seremban where he bought a watch and some shoes. Then he refused to pay any more. The other six partners arranged payments among themselves so that they were not owing each other money, leaving each with a personal debt due from the defaulter. Those due to adult men he paid off at the harvest, although only after a good deal of recrimination, but those due to three adolescents were still outstanding five years afterwards.

Even without cheating a villager may be forced to default. Some young men organized a *kutu* to buy musical instruments for a band. One of the participants was struck by sickness, which then hit one member of his family after another. He was therefore involved in expense as well as losing tapping days. He was forced to withdraw from the *kutu* though he was able to induce his half brother to take over two shares.

Although much concerned with shame (*malu*) in most things they do, Malay villagers do not stress reliability with money as a moral matter. The man who borrows money, especially from somebody richer, feels that his creditor was obliged to help him, rather than that he should be grateful himself. The known cheat can mix freely in village affairs and find yet other people to cheat.

The man entrusted with other people's money feels that a strong personal need of his own entitles him to misapply it, and what is more, his victims give weight to this view.

Such an attitude must have the same inhibiting effect on economic relations as the previously mentioned view that bargains can be adjusted should conditions alter to the disadvantage of one party, or expectations not be fulfilled.

CHAPTER VII

The Decline of the Traditional Political Organization

Once the main fabric of the social structure, matrilineal organization is now only one strand among many, and one that grows weaker with the passing of time. In this chapter I shall discuss the social forces which I believe have brought about the decline of the traditional organization, which has now gone so far that the term political is hardly applicable to the clan groupings. In the next chapter I shall describe some *adat* conflicts which I observed as illustrations of this process of decline, and of the present state of the *adat*.

The treaties between the Malay rulers and the British established a new political system which partly replaced, and partly existed alongside, the previous organization. Such coexistence of two political organizations is inherently unstable, because it means the attempt of two powers to exercise the same type of generalized control of the same population and territory.

In the Sultanates, where all authority was conceived to issue from the Sultan (Gullick, 1958) and political organization was territorial, there existed an administrative hierarchy, albeit primitive, which might be gradually made over into a modern administrative organization without any inevitable overt clash between the old and the new system. Such evolution has taken place in the Sultanates (Burridge, 1957). In Negri Sembilan, on the other hand, authority, broadly speaking, emanated from below, in the mass of the kinsmen, and traditional organization by kinship groups was not suited either to indirect rule, or to the giving of new definitions to existing political organization.

The absence of formal sanctions for adat in modern conditions

In some spheres of Government, functions previously carried out through *adat* have been directly taken over by the modern executive. The most important of these is the administration of justice and the use of force. Both the control of illegitimate expressions of violence, and the use of force in legitimate policy, are the exclusive monopoly of the administration. *Adat* is therefore without sanction in the last resort. Sanctions may be classified according to their severity (at least within one culture) and their degree of organization. The least severe and the least organized, are those relying on sentiment; the expression of dislike, ridicule, contempt, the loss of prestige. The most severe, and usually the most highly organized, are the formal imposition of definite punishments, especially the physical coercion of deviants. The latter I regard as ultimate sanctions.

It is these which the government monopolizes, and the unorganized forms have not proved, and could not be expected to prove, adequate to secure conformity to *adat*. Moreover, where interpretations of *adat* differ, it may be impossible to settle a dispute without an appeal to coercive sanctions, or even armed hostilities between the parties outside the system of organized sanctions.

THE NEW ADMINISTRATIVE ORGANIZATION

In the early days the activities of the administration were minimal, but in the course of time a comprehensive machinery of government has been created. Even were the traditional political system existing in something like its former strength, the growth of modern government would have dwarfed it, and by reducing its relative importance led to its absolute decline. In fact, the reaction between the two systems has been much more direct.

Organization on the basis of territory, with trained officials, is more efficient than the use of kin-groups. These, although they have a territorial base, are not residence groups, are small, and are distributed so as not to be easily grouped into useful administrative units. Also, the kinship groups are led by chiefs who are not trained, and who are only partly concerned with the affairs of their kin, for exogamy and matrilocality mean that a man's domestic and economic activities centre in another place. These chiefs, too, are subject to dismissal by their kin, regardless of their efficiency.

Government policy in the villages is made effective through a hierarchy of officials under the District Officer and the State Government.

Each *mukim* is in charge of a *penghulu*, with a number of village heads (*ketua kampong*) beneath him. The *penghulu* is a paid full-time official. The accord of the *Undang* is necessary for the appointment of a *penghulu*, one of the few direct ways he can influence the operation of the administration in his *luak*.

The *ketua* receives no pay, and only small allowances which are not adequate recompense for the time and energy he must spend if he is to do his job well. Since 1958 appointment to this office has been by election in the village, but before this there was no standard means of selection. In some cases elections were tried. In others attempts were made to establish the general choice by inquiries around the village; here the *penghulu*, as the main source of the District Officer's knowledge of village affairs and feeling, played an important part. The most common method was for the District Officer to appoint someone he considered suitable.

Prestige is the most important reward gained by a *ketua*. In no case was the *ketua* in possession of *adat* office, and in some cases he had no hope of receiving any, whether on account of his personal unpopularity with his kin, or of the position of his kin group. The *ketua* is a man of status. He will meet the District Officer and other officials in the course of his duties; they will greet him in the streets of the town and will attend his feasts. Significantly, a majority of the *ketua* resisted strongly the suggestion that the State Association, into which they are organized, should press for more adequate allowances, or even for wages. Their argument was that if they were paid they would cease to be private individuals helping the Goverment and become insignificant employees. The loss of prestige involved was greater than any salary they would be likely to receive could compensate them for.

Relations between *adat* chiefs and the *ketua* are often strained. The chiefs regard the *ketua* as usurpers, illegitimately claiming equality of status with them, and usurping their authority. To the *ketua* the *lembaga* is a nuisance. He does not help in the work of looking after his own kin, but expects deference, and to have his own way when an issue arises which affects him. Conflict may also arise between a chief and a *penghulu*, but in general it is the *ketua* who is the focus of resentment. The *penghulu* is more obviously the representative of government, and normally confines his concern with village affairs to his official capacity. Also, the *penghulu* will normally qualify for membership of the educated upper class, and will be more an official than a villager.

But the *ketua* is obviously a villager. In general terms, wealth, education, style of life, he will be similar to the *adat* chief, in *adat* the chief's inferior, and even within the Government the lowest grade of all, 'not even worth wages'. Yet the *lembaga* is faced with the galling fact that the *ketua* receives more attention from the administration (the upper class), and in many contexts even from the villagers, for he is the channel of communication with the administration.

In Kuala Pilah the chiefs have formed an association with the object of combatting the increased influence of the *ketua* and re-asserting their authority. In Jelebu similar attempts have been made on several occasions. A delegation of clan chiefs visited the District Officer in 1960 to discuss the matter, but they were not favourably received, and their opposition has been confined to threats to 'finish' the *ketua*.

The use of the term *dato empat* by *lembaga* to refer to the *ketua* is an interesting indication of relations between the two positions. This is the title of chiefs of alien groups, such as Minangkabau, attached to the main *adat* structure. Used of the *ketua* it brings them into the *adat* in an inferior position, and it is much resented by them. They have no business with the *adat*, they say. Their authority is their framed letter of appointment. The *Undang* is the *lembaga*'s chief and the District Officer is their chief. Let the clan chief bother with *adat*, the *ketua* is too busy looking after the village.

TECHNICAL SERVICES

Apart from general administration, many of the more specialized services of the executive can only be carried out on a much broader territorial basis than the lands of a sub-clan. Irrigation provides an apt illustration of such a service. Modern irrigation works affect the economy of all the population living along the banks of a river. While this area may conveniently fall within the boundaries of a *mukim*, it will certainly contain the lands of more than one clan. For example, although some fields use smaller tributary streams, the main source of irrigation in the *mukim* of Ulu Klawang is the River Klawang. From the point where it emerges from uninhabited secondary jungle, until it joins the river Triang near the district capital, the flow of the river is controlled by dams, irrigation channels and drains, constructed, maintained and administered by the Drainage and Irrigation Department. In the five miles of its course the river traverses the lands of five clans, the *waris* of Dato Amar Penghulu, formerly an independent chief on the borders of Sungai Ujong and Jelebu, the Waris Tiga Batu, Kemin, Batu Belang and Tanah Datah.

Rice was grown and the same source of water used, long before there was any Government to build big dams. But indigenous technology only allows small works to be undertaken, and except in very dry years, the activities of one village would not seriously affect the supply of water to downstream villages. In these circumstances the small kin-residence groups could make independent decisions on questions such as when to raise their dam. Now there are only two concrete dams for the whole valley. When these are opened the water reverts to the river bed, whether there are people who still want to use it or not. Two or three villagers, appealing to their neighbours and relatives, will receive more attention than they will from the Government. They are fully a part of the decision-making group, and a more significant part than they are of 'the public' which the Government has to consider. Control of dykes and banks has also passed out of the villagers' hands. Should a buffalo damage banks made by villagers the matter is settled in the village, but with government works a similar act of neglect is an offence involving fines.

To minimize the depredations of pests, to facilitate water control, and to allow the use of fields for pasture during the fallow season, it is desirable that rice cultivation follows a timetable standardized over as wide an area as possible.

Yet common timing is not easy to achieve, and this is not a new difficulty (Gullick, 1951 p. 46). In some areas nowadays much pressure is required before the peasants can be induced to start planting.

Even in the past, however, there was some coordination, and in this the chiefs played a major part. As the season drew near they would begin to press the villagers. Even if the clan chief lived elsewhere he would come, and by cajoling, and anger if necessary, move them to action.

Nowadays it is a rare *lembaga* who bothers with his clan's rice cultivation. Cultivation programmes have become a government concern. Annually the District Officer calls a meeting to decide the dates between which the various cultivation activities should be carried out. To this meeting, in addition to the *penghulu, ketua* and other officials concerned, all the clan chiefs will be invited. But only two or three will attend and they will play very little part in the discussion. Once the programme has been determined it is circulated in the villages, and it is the duty of the *penghulu* and *ketua* to see that it is followed. Wilful failure to conform is punishable with fines.

Two points for our discussion of *adat* emerge. This is another illustration of the need to develop institutions suited to the purposes of modern government, although there is no reason why the chiefs should not take a greater part in them. This is a matter bearing directly on the well-being of their kin, and one that is understandable to even the most traditionally oriented Malay.

We also see how chiefs, finding that they are losing authority and prestige, and that the administration carried on just as effectively whether they perform their duties or not, have been prepared to give up the exercise of leadership. To some extent the government is pushing out the *adat* authorities; but it is also filling a vacuum left where chiefs abdicate their duties.

In the villages today there is no clear legitimate authority. According to *adat* this should rest with chiefs and kin-group heads. But nowadays it is partly not recognized by some subjects and partly not exercized by some superiors. There is also lack of accord about the other grounds upon which the right to lead might be claimed, and no clear basis of relative ranking. The tension between the *ketua* and *adat* chiefs illustrates this situation, but people can also claim the right to lead because of wealth, occupation, education or religious qualification. The present indeterminate situation, in which the traditional status system no longer operates effectively to provide village leadership while a new one has yet to be established, encourages competition for prestige and power, and paralyses village capacity for cooperation.

THE JAPANESE OCCUPATION

The three years' occupation of Malaya by the Japanese before their surrender in 1945 had great consequences for the rate of social change in Jelebu, as elsewhere in Malaya. Documentary evidence concerning the period is scanty, and informants' accounts are very much biased by what they feel the observer wishes to hear, for the Occupation, and people's activities at that time, are still highly emotional topics. Even so, some conclusions may be drawn about the importance of the Occupation for social organization. Informants describe a pre-war society in which, on account of the solicitude of the British authorities for their treaty obligations, as well as the extraordinary force of the then *Undang*'s personality, the *adat* chiefs had much more power than they do now.

The *Undang* was held in awe by all the communities, indeed, this was still evident in the way he was spoken of more than a decade after his death. The impression of his power was strengthened by the extent to which the administration was prepared to humour him. Officers not personally acceptable to him were quickly transferred; 'twenty-fours hours' notice' the villagers relate. After one of his sons was killed in a playground accident, the newly opened Jelebu English school was closed, and it remained closed during his lifetime.

The villagers tell many stories of his behaviour to illustrate his forcefulness. For example, if he met two people riding on one bicycle he would stop his car and personally take them to the police station and insist that they be locked up. It was his practice to sit on the bench and help the magistrate judge cases. I have been told how he might insist on a higher fine than the magistrate had intended to impose, and then pay it himself, 'out of pity for his people'. Again, when I asked why few Jelebu people had planted rubber all over their homestead, as Malays will do elsewhere, I was simply told, 'the *Undang* would not allow it.'

I believe that in Jelebu the *Undang* was successfully able to slacken the pace of the decline of traditional power, and preserve some of the form, even when the objective foundations were dangerously undermined. Traditional values can influence behaviour long after the political organization with which they arose has decayed. The prestige of the *Undangship* and of the *adat* system, which even today are still considerable, together with the 'accident' of the personality of the *Undang* of the time, managed to temporarily dam forces, which burst forth all the more strongly, being concentrated in time, when the opportunity arose.

The Japanese provided this opportunity. To the villagers 'before the Japanese time' is the period when *adat* was strong, and 'the Japanese time' the period when the major decline began.

Broadly speaking, the Japanese, in their search for personnel to use in the administration, were solely concerned with ability to do the work. They showed no tenderness for the privileges of the *biduanda* or the *adat* chiefs. What is more their administration reached right down into the villages, creating official positions where none had existed before. For some individuals the new opportunities were welcome, and it should be realized that for the majority of Malays no question of collaboration arose. The Japanese replaced the British, and those who worked for them felt that they were receiving the recognition, or the opportunity, that they had previously been denied because of outworn kinship privileges.

The office of *ketua kampong* was first created in Negri Sembilan after the Occupation, and many of the holders of this office are men who first held minor official positions under the Japanese.

The return of the British with the Military Administration followed fifteen days of terror in which the Communists paid off some of the scores of the Occupation. These two weeks under the Three Stars seem to have frightened the Malays more than the whole period of Japanese rule. Confusion was general, in *adat* no less than elsewhere. Dato Abdullah had recently died. The Dato Mentri, saved in the nick of time from a more summary fate at the hands of the Communists, was arrested and convicted of collaboration.

The intrigue arising from the replacement of these two chiefs created enmities which have still not healed, but eventually order was restored. Even so, *adat* was not replaced on the pedestal from which it had been dislodged by the Japanese; nor, to tell the truth, does there seem any strong regret, or desire that it should be.

THE CONTROL OF LAND

I shall now discuss an important stage in the decline of chiefly authority where economic change, in the direction of the commercialization of the economy, reinforced in its results the consequences of Government policy.

During the nineteenth century the growth of a large-scale tin-mining industry gave new value to the clan jungle lands. Later the growing importance of commercial crops such as coffee and spices was another force working in the same direction. Jelebu did not, however, play much part in this cultivation. Much more important subsequently was the cultivation of rubber, but this crop appeared later than the developments now to be discussed, although it served to reinforce their consequences.

In 1891 the Government took over all land rights, in return making the *hasil tanah* payments to the *biduanda* already referred to. Titles were issued in respect of land already in use. This land was designated *tanah pusaka*, and was made subject, on devolution or sale, to the restrictions of the *adat* code. But this code was now administered by a magistrate and the clan chief was reduced to the role of technical witness. Instead of deciding cases he could now only give evidence as to the correct *adat* rule, the kinship connection between the disputants, and the previous history of the holding; the magistrate was not even bound to accept this.

Also, it was no longer to the clan chief that requests to open jungle land had to be made. Applications for land were considered by the District Office, in whose deliberations the question of whose *pusaka* the land had once been was not an issue. The *adat* restrictions did not apply to newly granted land, unless the owner wished to register his title as *tanah pusaka*. But with the growing commercialization of the economy, and the correspondingly smaller importance of subsistence *kampong* and rice-land products, it was precisely these new lands which were important and valuable.

Thus the effect of the restriction on the clan chiefs' control of land was reinforced by economic changes decreasing the importance of the land over which they still retained a measure of control.

THE RIGIDITY OF KIN GROUPING

The settlement of 1891 had an even more direct influence on the kinship organization. By giving pensions to those chiefly offices in existence at a given date, arbitrarily from the point of view of the kinship system, an artificial rigidity was introduced into it.

Although continual fission and segmentation were not a marked feature of the Negri Sembilan kinship system it did, nevertheless, adjust to changing circumstances, say to increasing population, by fission and the creation of new groups. Such adjustments can no longer take place because giving a limited number of pensions limits the number of chiefs. This is because the possession of a pension is a major criterion of the importance of an office, a sign of full and legitimate participation in the *pusaka*.

In Jelebu some groups have expanded beyond the size at which chiefs can reasonably be expected to perform their ceremonial duties, let alone maintain the personal contact with the affairs of the group which the system assumes.

This is so especially when groups have split away and established themselves some distance from the traditional home of the *perut*. Among the groups in the village where I lived there were two calling themselves *perut*. Neither had an *ibubapa*, for they had moved, in the latter years of the nineteenth century, from the *pusaka* of the *perut* Bemban *waris* Kemin, some thirty miles away. The *ibubapa* of the parent *perut* did not attend their ceremonies, and they had, to all intents and purposes, lost the right to participate in the election of chiefs. When the move is more recent propinquity of relationship enables ties to be maintained despite geographical distance. But after two or three generations the connection, while still acknowledged, becomes very vague.

This failure to reorganize offices to meet a new situation is not solely a matter of the limitation of pensions. The broad changes which have made it possible for people to live without a place in the *adat* structure are even more important. But the effect of the symbolic importance of a pension to a kinship office, and the limitations of their numbers to those existing in 1891, is an additional factor.

Reference may also be made to an economic change, which although affecting all relations between kin, does so especially when the distance between them is great. The villagers' reliance on regular tapping means that losing several days' tapping to attend a ceremony is a real hardship, and it is felt as a loss. Indeed, informants regarded the loss of even a day's tapping for this reason as a nuisance. In the past, on the other hand, subsistence production was more important, and the main source of cash was the man's rearing of buffalo for sale. It was then possible to devote several days to other activities without appreciable loss, especially as the traditional time for ceremonies is the lull after the harvest when there is also an abundance of grazing. As far as the case mentioned above was concerned, it was common for at least some of the men to make trips to Bemban for the purchase of cattle, using their kinship ties for economic purposes, and at the same time keeping them active.

THE ALIEN GROUPS

In the past the only immigrants were small numbers of culturally similar Indonesians or Malays who presented no challenge to the system. Today the position is very different. Chinese are more numerous in the District than Malays. Other races, although not great numerically, have their importance enhanced by disproportionate representation of their numbers in roles of economic or official importance. Differences of culture preclude the adoption of these people into Malay society, even if there were not barriers of hostility.

The presence of large numbers of people, living within the territorial boundaries of a political system, but not subject to its authority, serves to undermine the authority of that system. They provide a continual reminder of the limited powers of the leaders claiming authority, and the situation favours the development of some superordinate power to govern relations between those within and those without the system, in this case that of the administration whose authority is the same over all parties. Moreover the character of Malaysian immigration has itself changed. The largest group of newcomers are Mandahiling Batak who live in their own villages, endogamous (at least their women) speaking their own language, and with no place in the *adat* system, unlike other Malays who enter Jelebu either as transients (officials), or acquire some relationship to the local *adat* structure. The Mandahiling are despised as barbarous by the local Malays, but they are nevertheless seen as Muslim and related stock, and the fact that they too live independently of the *adat* system represents a greater challenge to its authority than does the independence of the Indians or Chinese.

Some of the Malay officials from outside Jelebu hold positions of high status, e.g. the present District Officer and Police Chief. These provide models with whom local Malays might well identify, personifying the fact that *adat perpateh* is a cultural alternative; in other words there are people of high status worthy of emulation who have nothing at all to do with *adat*.

THE DESIRE TO HOLD OFFICE

It often proves difficult to find a new incumbent for an office which does not carry a political pension. An *ibubapa* receives about $7.00 a month, which, although small, is still a sum worth having to the average villager, and, above all, is a symbol of the importance of the office.

Given the decline in the importance of office it is not surprising that there should be some individuals who feel that the rewards of office are not worth the trouble required. But, in view of the emotional value attached to *pusaka*, it is noteworthy that there are groups, and villagers at that, who are prepared to lose their *pusaka* through failing to provide even one candidate for a post.

In one example a group originating from Klang, 'attached' to the *waris* Kemin, had as their *pusaka* the office of one of the attendants to the clan chief. The nominal holder of this office was working outside Jelebu, and had therefore automatically forfeited it. But as no one else desired the post, and the *lembaga* did not complain, he was still regarded as holding it. Eventually the *Undang* ordered the *lembaga* to fill the post, and announced that if the original group could not provide a candidate they would lose the right. But no one could be found, 'who wants to go and sit on the *lembaga*'s verandah for three days (during the *hari raya* celebrations), just for the present of a couple of dollars? If there were a pension it would be different'.

So there is now another group living outside the *adat*. They still continue to observe many aspects of matrilineal custom, but as far as the political aspect of *adat* is concerned they have cut themselves off. Because of the decline in *adat* there is a loss of interest in the minor positions, and because these positions have no occupants yet a further decline results.

Where clan chieftainships are concerned the situation is different. These offices still carry enough prestige to make them desirable, and the pensions ($20.00 to $35.00) are regarded as a prize. So there are always people who would like to fill these positions. What is more difficult is to find someone who will perform the duties according to the traditional definition of the role. Ordinary villagers continually comment that the *lembaga* are not interested in their kin, only in their pensions. The *lembaga* should provide leadership for his *anakbuah*, and continually watch and guide their actions. Nowadays, for whatever reason, they largely confine themselves to attending the ceremonies of the wealthier members of their group.

CONCLUSION

The decline of *adat* as a political system has been attributed to the growth of modern administration. Government has robbed *adat* of adequate sanction thus gradually releasing the deviant pressures contained by any system of social control. Also, the imperatives of efficient administration have required that the traditional authorities be supplemented, or supplanted, by new organization. Sometimes this has resulted in direct competition with the *adat* system, sometimes merely in its being ignored. Change has consisted in one system replacing another, not in a gradual modification of the old.

Political change is an element in the process of general cultural change which provides the setting within which the analysis of structural problems is carried out.

The Malay villager is subject to many cultural pressures which suggest alternatives to traditionally accepted patterns of behaviour. Schools, films, the radio, the example of alien groups, and of the more successful members of his own society, all present models of behaviour differing from those his father would have accepted as natural.

The appeal of new ways is enhanced by their identification with wealth and prestige, for the new ways are the criteria which distinguish a member of the modern elite class of officials from the peasantry. The villager is aware of the modern influences in the life of the upper class, and though he criticizes them he himself has an insatiable desire for the products of modern industry. A bicycle, a sewing machine, a radio, are common possessions in the village.

The appeal is even greater to the young. For the adventurous few modern ways suggest really radical notions, such as choosing one's own spouse. or education and a career for a girl; for any youth they provide a charter for revolt against the older generation. For the elders have not validated their claims to wisdom with any tangible success, a clear proof that they do not understand the modern world, and should give way to those who do.

It is not necessary to analyse this general process of culture change into its constituent elements and consider the consequences of each for the total pattern. No one element seems to have been especially important; it is rather, as the Malays see it, a question of competition between two ways of life.

Attitudes of challenge and defence are often expressed. The villager feels himself threatened and regards new culture patterns as part of that threat. More general than rejection is the notion that adjustments must be made, although as to what adjustments the villager does not know. Many villagers when discussing the future seem sure of only one thing. There will be many more changes, and the Malay will be the loser from them all.

CHAPTER VIII

Some Recent Adat Disputes

I shall now describe three disputes which occurred during my period of fieldwork, or shortly afterwards. The first concerns clan office, the second *adat* and religion and the third marriage regulation. The first and second examples involved the whole *luak*, the third really concerned only one clan. The number of examples given could be multiplied many times over for disputes, large and small, are a constant feature of *adat perpateh* today, so much so that the *adat* quarrels of Negri Sembilan have become a source of amusement for other Malays.

In the second chapter I mentioned a case where a clan chief, chosen and installed by his clan, was not accepted by the *Undang* and Council of Eight, and hence could not be properly appointed. This conflict was not one which could be resolved according to *adat*. The *waris* were insisting on their right to choose their own chief, a basic principle of the kinship political system. But this conflicted with the other important principle which invests the *Undang* with a measure of independent authority outside the *adat*, and also with the rule that all appointments of clan chiefs must be approved by him and the Council of Eight.

In the past this conflict could have been resolved by armed struggle between the parties. It need not even have been necessary for fighting to take place; the mere knowledge that it could would be a powerful force making for compromise. In modern conditions such a conflict of principle could be resolved if the Administration, which now monopolizes the legitimate use of force, was prepared to make a decision between the parties and enforce it.

The *waris* appealed to both the District Officer and the State Government, but both declined to intervene, except as mediators, in a matter of Malay Custom.

The *waris* also wrote to all the members of the Council of Eight respectfully asking for clarification of the faults of their candidate, or of the installation ceremony, and how these might be rectified. The chiefs either ignored the letter, or let it be known that they could not receive it, for to have done so would have implied some recognition of the claims of the *waris* and their chief, and would also have been an offence against the *Undang*, setting oneself up as an authority in the dispute independently of him and the Council of Eight.

At first there were two clear objections against the candidate, as well as vaguer assertions that the ceremony of his installation was not properly carried out. First that he had tuberculosis, and secondly that his wife was an *anak china* (bought as a baby from her parents and reared as a Malay). In answer to the first of these objections the candidate was examined in Seremban Hospital and produced evidence that his lungs were clear. The second was met with the retort that his wife had been reared as a Malay since she was a few days old, and hence was indistinguishable from a 'real Malay'. But as these objections were excuses overcoming them did not advance the case at all.

For several months it seemed that the problem would remain unresolved indefinitely, and since it is no longer the *Undang* and the clan chiefs who govern the *luak* there was no pressing reason why it should not. The manner of the solution of the conflict is revealing also. Over a year after the chief had been installed by his clan, the *Undang* received him at the *Balai*, and he was at last fully appointed. Very briefly the *Undang* changed his mind.

For as long as both parties were firm in their resolve it was a conflict for which there was no structural solution under modern conditions. The Government, which defines the context within which these disputes take place, forbids the use of violence, and yet will not settle disputes which have become intractable. A by-product of these disputes, which are themselves a reflection of the present state of *adat*, is a further weakening of *adat*, which cannot operate at all at inter-clan level during such a disturbance.

The Government does not always adopt such a passive role. For much of 1958 there was another major dispute in Jelebu. Tension first became marked during the Fasting Month of 1957. Then for the first time officials (*amil*) were appointed to collect the Muslim charity/tax of *Zakat Fitrah*.

To the villagers *fitrah* was not a Government tax, but a charity to be given with proper ceremonial to whomsoever the donor judged fit to receive it (from amongst those qualified under Muslim law). Though it was not part of the matrilineal *adat*, the traditional arrangements for paying *fitrah* were nevertheless regarded as *adat*, and they were certainly an important way of recognizing the services of those who carried out religious duties for the villagers throughout the year. Every feast requires prayers, and not every villager knows them. Each village has its recognized *orang alim*, pious and knowledgeable men, and they are invited to occasions where prayers are needed. The payment of *fitrah* is one of the ways in which this help is recognized.

The villager typically stresses the spirit behind religious acts, rather than formal adherence to rules. Thus the policeman, who receives a receipt for $1.00 deducted from his pay as *fitrah*, has not really paid, for paying *fitrah* should take place in the proper context of a feast, and it should be given with sincerity (*ikhlas*) to someone the donor feels should receive it. Within the village nearly everyone, no matter how poor, paid *fitrah*, either in cash, or with a bushel of rice for every member of the family. Where a feast would be too expensive the poor villager made his payments at a feast given by a richer relative or neighbour.

In 1957 a few paid the money to the *amil*, some paid twice, once to the *amil* and once in village style, and the majority ignored the new arrangements. The following year the Department of Religious Affairs made preparations for a more inclusive and better organized collection, with penalties for those who refused to pay. In addition an Ordinance was introduced which was seen by the villagers as destroying *adat*. Besides the provisions concerning *fitrah paksa* (compulsory *fitrah*) much greater powers were to be given to the *kadi* in matters of inheritance and family law, and all *wakaf* (dedicated religious property) was to be transferred to the control of the Department of Religious Affairs. The villagers complained bitterly that they were to be made to pay for burial in their ancestral graveyards.

Much of their resentment was directed against the *Undangs* as signatories of the Ordinance. The clan chiefs did not want to take any action at first, but they were led by the strength of feeling among their *anakbuah* to meet the *Undang* to discuss the changes and to protest against the proposed infringements of *adat*. My informants among the chiefs stressed that at this point they did not feel that they were attacking either the *Undang* or the *kadi*.

They were, however, angered at the reception the *Undang* gave them. When he had finished speaking one of the chiefs said that such harsh words would require that the *Undang taboh melukut* (give a feast to redress his wrong, similar to the *timbang salah* feast of ordinary people). The *Undang* refused, and subsequently also endeavoured to call together the *ibubapa* over the heads of the clan chiefs, a serious wrong given the emphasis in *adat* on following the proper channels.

The *lembaga* organized a meeting at the Mesjid Kuala Dulang, a mosque connected with legends of the original founder of Jelebu and the *keramat*[1] of the *luak*. There, in the presence of several hundred witnesses the clan chiefs decided to dismiss the *Undang*, took an oath to that effect, and signed a document. A letter was sent to the Chief Minister of Negri Sembilan informing him of their decision.

According to Jelebu *adat* a unanimous decision of the Council of Eight is sufficient to dismiss the *Undang*. But the *Undang*, alone among the *adat* chiefs, also has a position in the modern constitution, and to be effective his dismissal requires the concurrence of the Administration. To the villagers this means, above all, withdrawing his political pension, and the UNDANG JELEBU car plate.

On this occasion the Administration gave wholehearted support to the *Undang*, and was able to induce two of the *lembaga* to change their position. The other six held fast, led by the chiefs of the *waris silsila*, until early 1959, when some others reaffirmed their loyalty to the *Undang*. Hostile criticism attributed this defection to the Government's decision to cease pension payments to the dissident *lembaga*. This may well have been a factor, but there was also despair of succeeding in the face of the Government's obvious intention to retain the *Undang*, and the reemergence of respect for the *Undang* after the initial anger engendered by his remarks had cooled.

This case shows clearly the strength of the villagers' loyalty to *adat* and how Islam is connected with *adat* in their minds. It was the anger of their kinsmen which first induced the *lembaga* to complain, and further evidence of the strength of popular feeling was provided by the size of the gathering in the mosque.

---

[1] *Keramat* is used of people, places and objects with supernatural qualities. People vow offerings to *keramat* in return for fulfilled wishes.

My own impression, formed during visits to Jelebu, was of widespread support for the Council of Eight. Even those people who were not prepared to support a move for the removal of the *Undang* (mainly members of his own clan), disliked the new provisions for religion and wanted a return to the previous position without changing the *Undang*.

Both this and the earlier example illustrate the meaning of non-interference by the Administration in matter of Malay custom and religion. To the Administration *adat* is a tiresome complication in the smooth operation of Government. Even if legally unable to intervene the power of the administration is so predominant and pervasive that considerable influence can be exerted on the course of an *adat* dispute. On the other hand, the feelings of the villagers about *adat* make any major dispute a hindrance to the carrying on of ordinary affairs in the District. Accordingly, the Government uses its influence to lessen disruption, and much of the time this means supporting not *adat* but the established office holders, especially the *Undang*. The place of the *Undang* on the State Executive Council is also relevant here.

These two cases refer to situations which would have involved, even under traditional conditions, the resort to non-legitimate, or abnormal, means. For while the use of force as an ultimate argument is clearly implicit in the traditional structure, situations where it must be resorted to represent a mal-operation of that structure (here I refer to conflict between major elements of the political structure, not the physical discipline of deviants). Under present conditions the administration's monopoly of the use of force, and its refusal to settle major crises, give rise to the possibility of paralysis of the whole *adat* structure, and such paralysis, even temporary, serves to hasten further its general decline.

My next case falls fully within the bounds of *adat* law. I refer to a marriage of matrilineal cousins, a very serious breach of exogamy, which would have been inconceivable, at least in the way it took place, a decade or two ago. This case is 'normal', unlike the first two examples, in that it is an eventuality covered by the *adat* code and the sayings; on the other hand, it is clearly 'abnormal' in the shocked responses it drew from the villagers.

A distinction is made between incest which offends the tenets of Islam as well as *adat*, and marriages which while forbidden by *adat* are permissible under Islam. For the former crime the penalty was death, although this might be commuted to outlawry. For the latter it was confiscation of property and exile, although if the guilty parties divorced they might be allowed to *timbang salah* and pay a fine. From Jempol I have learned of another possibility, that one of the couple might be adopted by another group, so that the marriage would then be permissible, and there are sayings in support of this.[1] This possibility was not, however, raised in discussions of the following case which I heard.

The marriage was the outcome of arrangement between the two families, particularly the respective fathers, with the mother's brother (real to groom and classificatory to bride), the main authority and primarily responsible under *adat*, as a willing accessory.

According to neighbouring village opinion the main incentive for the match was a desire that the groom's earnings as schoolmaster should benefit a member of the group rather than an outsider. This explanation, although formulated in an unduly mercenary way, certainly accords with the usual reasoning behind marriage arrangements.

The male principals, who were all in Government employment, had received modern education, and were disposed to regard the *adat* as old-fashioned nonsense. Even so, there was great opposition and disquiet amongst most of the villagers in the kin-group. They were faced with the alternatives of breaking off relations with the families preparing the wedding, or of accepting the responsibility of helping, and so sharing in the ridicule which the marriage was sure to arouse. (Such marriages are referred to as the conduct of *hewan* animals, or cattle, although the villagers are aware that they are common throughout the Peninsula and allowed by Islam.)

Two factors are especially relevant in the choice facing individuals opposed to the wedding. Firstly, in a number of contexts, but especially in ceremonial, the individual's dependence on his kin-group is very great. Only kin can be relied on to carry out the work which a feast entails. Thus the choice was seen as between reluctant participation, and being left without help when faced with one's own weddings, circumcisions and deaths. Secondly, because of their occupation and education, all the male proposers of the scheme were men of high status outside *adat*, at

---

[1] Personal communication from Mr. A. Kahar Bador.

least in the village context. Apart from their prestige, ties with a person occupying official position can be of practical value to a villager. Their status inclined the kin to follow them, albeit reluctantly, rather than risk a quarrel. Especially so as neither the kin-group, nor the *orang semanda*, contained individuals of nearly equivalent status, or of sufficiently forceful personality, to provide a leader to express their misgivings.

The couple were wed according to Muslim rites and a small feast given. Save for the relationship of the couple this is in accordance with local practice. Where there are practical reasons for delaying the full ceremony it is quite common for an engaged couple to be married in this way. They are married, but they are expected to observe almost as close avoidance as they did before the marriage. Full marital relations must await the completion of the *adat* ceremony.

The clan chief's reaction was to order the couple to be divorced and a fine paid. This order was ignored, and there the matter rested for there was no way to enforce conformity if the people were not amenable to moral pressure.

Modern attitudes do more than lessen feelings of guilt about infringing the *adat*; they provide a positive sanction for behaviour which can be seen as 'freeing the Malay people from the bonds of outworn custom which make them a backward group even in their own country'. The deviant can picture himself as a pioneer of progress; these people did, as they were, of course, entitled to do.

Willingness to defy custom has more causes than the lack of formal sanctions. It is now possible to live outside *adat* in a way that was impossible when it provided the political system. Losing one's *pusaka* now has little more than emotional significance, and this will have little weight with a man who is deriving his values, and fixing his ambitions, on supra-village society. The daily contacts of people occupying official positions are in a sphere where the status claims of *adat* chiefs are not recognized, and where they can ignore the criticisms and hostility that their actions may give rise to in the village. They have no respect for the opinions of ignorant villagers, nor do they depend on them, since they are in salaried employment.

In the past the refusal to carry out the *lembaga*'s order would have brought severer penalties, and the punishment of the *lembaga* himself, as he would have been held responsible for the actions of his kin. Today continued minor breaches going unpunished have given *adat* an optional character, and led to a situation in which people are prepared to commit one of the most serious offences.

Approximately a year later the other major marriage ceremonial was carried out. It was felt necessary to eliminate all items of ceremonial and regalia which derive their significance from *adat*. This was partly to avoid mockery and accusations of presumption, but in any case, it would have been difficult to use ceremonials which stress the relations between two groups when the relationship between the people concerned was so close.

The ceremony was therefore much attenuated. But this is a general feature of weddings throughout Malaya, where stress is increasingly laid on one feast which should be as magnificent as possible. Also, in keeping with the justification found for the wedding, a greater place than usual was found for Islam. There were several performances of Arabic songs, and recitations from the Koran, by a religious teacher and a mixed group of his pupils coming from a neighbouring District. These took the place of *Maulud Nabi*, a recitation of the life of the Prophet, which is traditionally given the night before a wedding. Like all other traditional religious practises *maulud* is closely bound up in the villagers' minds with *adat* as a part of the old ways, and is one of the things which religious teachers of modern bent often criticize. Also it requires the mobilization of a group of men familiar with the words and technique. These older men, of more traditional outlook, would not have wished to be associated with such a wedding.

An important question is who was present at the wedding. Any relative, or any *adat* chief, who attends a ceremony implies his approval of what is being done, and shares the responsibility for anything that might be wrong with it. Other guests show approbation, or, in this case especially, at least that their desire to be on good terms with the givers of the feast is stronger than any criticism they might feel.

Neither the *ibubapa* of the subclan nor any of his siblings or affines was present. Since they belonged to a different extended family in the subclan considerations of mutual help in the future were of less importance to them than resentment and shame at the disgrace suffered by their *perut*. Had any of the immediate kin of the *ibubapa* attended it would have been tantamount to his own appearance, and hence condonation, of the affair. Nowadays an *ibubapa* can avoid responsibility for the remoter members of his subclan, as he cannot be reasonably expected to control them, but not for his own extended family.

Most of the other clan chiefs were conspicuous by their absence. Conspicuous because it was to be expected that several of them would be present at any wedding given by people of high status. On this occasion only two *lembaga* appeared. One, the bride's father's father, had gone before the majority of guests arrived. Of the other, it was said that he came from some distance and was not aware of the relationship of the bride and groom until too late.

Nevertheless there was a large and distinguished gathering. Government officials, schoolteachers, the United Malay Nationalist Organization leaders, and men of substance in the villages with no *adat* rank to guard, attended in numbers, providing a satisfactory affirmation of their hosts' status and a justification of their decision to follow personal preference rather than the rules of *adat*.

According to informants this was only the second wedding of its kind to occur in Jelebu. Because of the status of the main actors they were favourably placed to carry out their plan. Even so, had there been any male relatives of comparable authority who were traditionally oriented it would probably not have taken place. The only other known case of a marriage of this kind occurred during the reign of Dato Abdullah. He drove the couple out, reportedly saying that since the marriage was permitted by religion he would not allow them to divorce, but that since it was not allowed by *adat* they must leave the society. Establishing themselves in what was then remote jungle, the couple prospered materially, but never had any children, a sign, at least to village opinion, of supernatural disapproval.

The whole planning of the marriage was complicated by the fact that traditional procedures and definitions of obligation are in terms of matrilineal kinship, and could no longer be applied in a marriage where the couple were so related. The principals announced at one stage that they were not going to use *adat* at all, and were simply going to invite guests and ask for help on the basis of neighbourhood. Later however, they decided to rely on the assistance of the kin and affines who would normally help with a ceremonial and to invite outsiders simply as guests. Many of the minor actors complained of the heavy burden of work, and the difficulty of working out one's obligations, when the affair is within one *perut*. Although the planners of this marriage departed from *adat* in one important respect they nevertheless wanted to retain it in others, and to benefit from traditionally defined obligations of help and support. For smooth arrangement a greater break with tradition was required, but this would have meant the loss of legitimacy adhering to obligations defined according to *adat* (despite the clash with *adat* the kin and *orang semanda* were fulfilling traditional obligations to assist), and also that people would not have known what to do unless they were explicitly taught.

These difficulties were not wasted upon the villagers among the guests, who have a very practical appreciation of the problems involved in giving a large feast. Many of them remarked on them, and expressed their determination to retain the old ways.

CHAPTER IX

Family and Domestic Groups (1)

Where matrilineal tracing of descent is combined with exogamy and a matrilocal residence rule, kinship groupings are not those of domestic and community organization. Given male predominance, a universal feature of human society, it follows that any society following these three rules is faced with potential conflict in areas of social organization where groupings based on descent and those based on common residence and domestic interests overlap.

In Negri Sembilan the ideal solution to the 'matrilineal puzzle' (Richards, 1950, p. 246) is the complete subordination of a man to his wife's kin-group. The sources of strain, however, continue to exist, and the superiority of the *tempat semanda* in the *tempat semanda–orang semanda* relationship depended to a great extent on the sanctioning of this relationship as part of the traditional political organization.

The decline of *adat perpateh* as a political system may therefore be expected to alter the balance between kin and domestic groupings in favour of the latter.

NUCLEAR FAMILY

The nuclear family of husband, wife and dependent children is the most common form of domestic grouping, and also the major social unit in day-to-day living.

Husbands attempt to build their own house as soon as possible after the birth of their first child (which ideally will occur within a year of marriage), and to establish their own family of procreation as an independent unit. This is a legitimate goal to which the wife's father should give such help as he can. This help is seen not as help to the son-in-law but rather as an attempt to establish his daughter securely by providing her with a house, in the same way as she has been provided with a husband, and (ideally) land for the sustenance of herself and her children.

People continually refer to the notion of paying debts to one's children. These debts are the duty of all Muslim parents to arrange for the religious education, circumcision (or a comparable rite for girls), and marriage of their children. This religious duty does not depend on, or imply, any definite reciprocity from the child. Islam has much to say about a child's duty towards its parents, but this is not as precise and formal as the three debts of a parent.

There is a significant difference in the relative weight of the three debts to sons and daughters respectively. For a son his pre-paration for Islam (education and circumcision) is more important than marriage. Informants frequently commented that you cannot make a man marry unless he wants to. For a daughter religious education and subincision are light matters. The former usually consists merely of a little instruction in reading the Koran from her father at home, and the latter is usually not considered worth any special ceremony, but fitted in when convenient, as a minor adjunct to a brother's or cousin's circumcision. A daughter's marriage, however, is a great responsibility, and a daughter who has to be found a spouse is a source of worry to her parents. For a youth circumcision, taking place during the early teens, is the *rite de passage* marking the change to adult status. For a girl the important rite is her marriage. Although the onset of puberty shows that she is nubile, and so may affect her parents' attitude

TABLE 2.   Household Composition of a Village
(*Total number of households* 71)

Household Type	Number of Cases
Nuclear Family*	33
Nuclear Family & Wife's Father	1
Nuclear Family & Wife's Mother	3
Joint Family	6
Single Individual	3
Husband, Wife & Grandchildren	6
Mother & Dependent Children	6
Mother, Children & Stepfather	11

* Husband–wife households are counted as nuclear families.

towards her, it does not mark such an important transition in social status as marriage.

When a son has married his life is very much his own, but the 'debt' to a daughter, although formally discharged when she is married, implicitly also involves a duty to see her as securely provided for as possible. The concern shown over a daughter's marriage makes it seem a parents' major problem, and this is an accurate reflection of the relative vulnerability of the sexes to domestic misfortune.

When established in a separate dwelling the nuclear family is the main producing and consuming unit of the society. During the interim period between marriage and the birth of a child, when there is a joint household with the wife's parents, there is no fixed rule for the division of expenses. If anything the father should bear more, but the son-in-law must contribute as generously as he can, and provide some items, such as clothes for his wife, on his own.

Wage earning outside the village has long been common in Negri Sembilan. The Emergency enormously increased the opportunities for wage employment and now a very large proportion of young men, and their families, are living outside the village. A village of 70 houses may contain no young man between about 18 and 25 years of age, but it is not possible to give a precise percentage, as there is quite a marked variation between villages, apparently explained by the importance of connections in opening the way for youth to leave the village. With these wage-earning families the rule is best described as neolocality. As soon as the young man is given quarters, or can rent a house, he will send for his wife, and the independent household may therefore be established sooner than it would be in the village. But leave will be spent mainly with the wife's parents, for the wage-earner will not want to build a house in the village to stand empty most of the time. In this discussion I shall be concerned with these service families only in so far as I observed them when on leave, or when a wife returned to bear a child or to wait for her husband to get a house after posting to a new area.

THE FAMILY ROLES

Before discussing institutions such as marriage and divorce I wish to describe the general pattern of relationships within the family.

(a) Husband-wife

The attributes stressed as desirable for a successful marriage relate to the ability of the couple to cooperate successfully in the division of labour by sexes.

A woman's work is first of all the ordinary domestic duties of the household. In addition the wife often assumes the main burden of work in the ricefields, and industry here is highly valued. A wife should also possess enough rice land for the family's subsistence needs (although an increasing proportion do not) and a house site.

Men also work in the ricefields, and some of them are very industrious, but this is something extra about a good husband rather than an essential quality. Many men plead their work rubber tapping as a sufficient excuse for not giving any significant help in rice cultivation. It is the provision of an adequate cash income that is the husband's main responsibility, and the main indicator of a good husband in public judgement.

An intimate relationship persisting over the years naturally has a marked emotional aspect, but this is not recognized by the people in their ideology of marriage. Parents should love their children, but affection is not necessary between husband and wife. They are partners in a joint enterprise which will persist for as long as it is mutually profitable. Displays of affection between men and women are thought comical or disgusting, and may give rise to the suspicion that one partner has bewitched the other. A man is not criticized if he shows grief, or even weeps, at the death of a child or parent, but the loss of a wife should be accepted calmly in the spirit that one can always look for another. If one spouse dies, or a couple divorce, people immediately begin to consider the possibility of remarriage, and to refuse a suitable offer is regarded as unreasonable.

A woman is not supposed to play any part in the major affairs of the society, but should contentedly confine herself to caring for her husband and children. She should accept the decisions of her male kin, or her husband without hesitation. This is the picture presented by the formal institutions: women must keep modestly to the background. Should a woman refuse to accept the limitations of her role she is at first regarded with amusement, and then with increasing indignation. Only if she is prepared to be regarded as 'three-quarters', i.e. mentally unbalanced, can a woman escape the strict requirements of modesty. Both men and women say that women 'cannot understand affairs'. Women who step right out of their traditional role, say as schoolteachers, or leaders of Kaum Ibu (women's branch of the UMNO), are regarded with considerable suspicion and some hostility by the peasants.

Such is society's image of itself, and in some situations it is accurate enough. But even if not formally recognized, woman's role in the direction of society is very important. Men do not make decisions concerning their families without prior discussion with their wives, and in this discussion the wife may well be the dominant party. Even in public discussion, where women may not participate (although older women may call out comments during pre-ceremonial kin gatherings *berkampong*) the opinions which a man expresses may well have been formed by discussion with his wife in the privacy of evening.

Economic interests are merged in the partnership of marriage to only a limited extent. Within the household there is a clear division of property between the husband, wife, and even children. This will not be apparent in the day to day use of the property, but it is nevertheless a factor affecting management decisions.

Women wish to accumulate land registered in their own name, or gold. They want some provision for their future security in a society where divorce is regarded as an ever present possibility. Also a husband should be prepared to give property to his wife, whenever he is able, as an earnest that he is not contemplating divorce, and for the maintenance of his children should he ever do so. A man may secure almost the same result by registering property in the name of a child, which ensures that it will not be misused by the mother, or any future stepfather, during the child's minority. Rice land and homestead are particularly appropriate for a woman to own, and for a man to buy such property, and register it in his own name, would be seen as a sure sign that he was planning a divorce.

(b) Parent-child

In the family the authoritarian element essential in the parent-child relationship is reduced to a minimum. Punishment is rare, and makes a parent run the risk of being considered cruel. The whims of children are satisfied as far as possible, even at the expense of the family as a whole: for example the continual demands for cakes and sweets which can, with a large family of small children, make serious inroads into a small budget.

Until the age of six or seven years there is little distinction made in the treatment of boys and girls. Parents are equally pleased with the birth of a son or a daughter, 'whatever God gives'. If a couple already have a daughter they would like a son, and vice-versa. Having a daughter first is a good thing, for she will be able to help later with her younger siblings. But there is nothing to approach the Chinese concern with male offspring, and this points to an interesting characteristic of the Negri Sembilan system. For a society in which the major groups are recruited by unilineal descent there is very little concern with lineage. The ancestors have no specific importance to their descendants, and in the same way there is very little concern with the perpetuation of a descent line. A daughter is desired as a comfort in old age, and as a source of grandchildren to enjoy. A son cannot be these things as he will move away on marriage, and his children will be seen only occasionally. A daughter may also be desired so that property will not pass to strangers. But all these evaluations of sons and daughters may be expressed by fathers too; they are family rather than kinship sentiments. A kin-group is its living members; there is no stress on it as an unbroken chain ascending into the past, and descending into the future for ever if possible.

As the children grow older distinctions are made approximating to the appropriate adult roles. As she approaches puberty a girl is increasingly confined to the household, while a son will gain increasing independence and freedom. A girl is fully integrated into the economy of the household, helping her mother with domestic tasks, although, for modesty, not going to the ricefields. With a son the situation is quite different. As an adolescent he can make as much money, rubber tapping, as an adult with family responsibilities, but only in exceptional circumstances, for example if his mother is a widow, will he make more than small and irregular contributions to the household expenses. The adolescent youth passes his time in the company of his peers, a band of youths sleeping in each other's houses or in the prayer house, as convenient, and eating where they are invited.

Before starting as an independent tapper, a boy commonly spends a period helping someone else, collecting scrap, and

cleaning latex cups, for a small fee. I know of no case in which a
boy worked with his father in this way. This is partly because
the boy wants money and he cannot expect his father to pay for
such help. But there is also a change in the quality of the father–son
relationship as the son grows older. The Malay father is even more
indulgent than the mother when the children are young, for the
mother must enforce a modicum of discipline. As a son moves
out of the restricted environment of the home his father will
attempt to see that he turns out a proper man, and therefore to
control him. During a son's adolescence and early adulthood
relations with the father are often poor, improving only later
when they meet almost as equals. Probably the demand for
discipline after almost complete freedom as a child is particularly
difficult for a son to accept. Daughters, gradually disciplined from
an early age, are not faced with such a problem of adjustment.
The mother, no longer having to control an unruly child, can
give indulgence freer rein, and it is she who acts as a buffer between father and son when tension becomes pronounced.[1]

SIBLING RELATIONSHIPS

There are three named positions. *Abang* elder brother. *Kakak*
elder sister, and *adek* younger brother or sister. Among siblings
authority rests with the elder, but the older sibling is expected
to be indulgent towards his *adek*. When the younger sibling is
old enough to understand, respect should be accorded elder
siblings, but until then the elder sibling must show great for-
bearance. Frequently observed regressive behaviour on the part
of a recently displaced youngest child leads me to believe the
change disturbing.

In adolescence and later older siblings exercise great influence,
and I was impressed by the way in which men, who were felt
to have behaved wrongly or foolishly, would accept rebuke or
advice from older siblings which would have been angrily rejected from others. I also noticed how village leaders preferred
to express warning criticism to an older sibling rather than directly
to a deviant.

The eldest brother and sister often have a special, quasi-parental

---

[1] Freudian theory is obviously relevant to the discussion of these relationships, but it
falls outside my competence.

relationship with their younger siblings, and they alone[1] have a special designation, with *long* added to *abang* or *kakak*. If the eldest sibling has borne a lot of responsibility the special position of *kak long* or *abang long* is marked. But the eldest may not be the dominant sibling, and then the special position will be confined to the title, and even that may not be used.

There is no arrangement for unique succession. This is in keeping with the previously remarked lack of discrimination between sons and daughters in terms of their importance for the descent line. There is no concern with the transmission of corporate rights to the next generation which would make such arrangements functional. Property passes to all daughters, and should this result in its division into small lots, it is unfortunate only because it may mean hardship for them, not because descent group property is being dispersed. Office rotates, so whatever office the descent group may have at a given moment will probably be in another extended family or in another *perut* in the next generation. There are no descent-based rituals, and so no ceremonial duties or objects, responsibility for which must be transmitted.

STEP-RELATIONS

Although I did not find the very high levels of divorce which characterize Malay society as a whole (see below) divorce is still common. Primitive medical beliefs and practices lead to many deaths. But divorced and bereaved spouses normally marry again within a short time. It is therefore a common experience for a child to find itself with a stepfather. But not with a stepmother. Children remain with their mother after divorce. Even if the marriage ended with the death of the mother the children will be reared by her kin rather than go with their father to his kin, or to his new wife's house. This follows *adat*, but there is a more general theme in Malay culture expressed in stories, songs and now films, which sees having a stepmother as the cruellest fate which could befall anyone. It is said that with the best will in the world a stepmother will favour her own children, and that most of them will be actually cruel.

In other parts of Malaya a father is recognized as having a right to some of the children of a marriage; for example, informants in

---

[1] Parent's siblings are differentiated terminologically according to birth order with the suffixes *Sulong* eldest, *Ngah* middle, *Chik* younger than parent, and *Chu* youngest. The *long* in *Kakak Long* or *Abang Long* is an abbreviation of *sulong*.

Province Wellesley and Perak stated that the mother takes her sons and the father takes his daughters. In such a case it will be said that the daughters 'followed' their father. But this must not be taken literally; in nearly all cases that informants could recall, it meant the informal adoption of the child by one of the father's female kin, usually his mother or his sister. The former wife's kin (should she have died) will resist strongly any proposal to take the children to live with their father's new wife, and even the father's kin will recognize that this is likely to cause suffering to the child. In Negri Sembilan the father does not even have this right. I know of no case where the father kept any of his children after a divorce, and only two where the father kept any of them after his wife's death. In one of these the father did not remarry for some years and his daughter lived with him in his mother's house, while her brother stayed with the dead wife's mother. When the father eventually remarried the daughter joined her brother. In the second case, again, the husband has not yet re-married and has brought back his newly married eldest daughter to look after the children. The grandparents, however, are not satisfied with this arrangement and are determined to take the children should he remarry.

Having a stepfather is not seen as a hardship of the same magnitude. Primary responsibility for the care of the children rests with the mother and she can ensure that they are equally treated. Even if he feels differently about his own children and his step-children a man does not have the same opportunity to discriminate that a stepmother has, and what is more, can only do so in public ways. He might give his stepchildren inferior schooling, or less expensive feasts at wedding or circumcision, or arrange inferior marriages to those of his own children; he can give his children presents and not his stepchildren. But the community will notice and criticize, if not to his face, and here the fear of *malu* (shame), the hypersensitiveness to what other people may be thinking about one, becomes important.

All stepfathers I observed in Jelebu seemed to make no distinction between their own and their stepchildren, whether in material treatment or fondness and emotional interest shown in them.

ADOPTION (Djamour, 1952, Rosemary Firth, 1943)

Full adoption, giving the child full jural rights as if it were the real child of its adopted parents, is rare. There is only one such case in the 71 households tabulated in Table 2. I know of other cases, but not more than one or two in a village. As far as a local Malay child is concerned, adoption outside the subclan would be difficult, involving the consent of many people whose rights were potentially affected, and to allow a child to leave the subclan would also seem shameful, as if there were no one among its kin who was prepared to rear it. Within the subclan there is no need for formal adoption, for adoption simply implies giving more content to an already existing classificatory relationship.

There is no full adoption of Malays because there are no Malay children to adopt. Most Malays desire children so much that were a parent forced, or willing, to part with a child there would always be a relative anxious to take it and rear it.

Full adoption occurred when a Malay took (usually bought) a Chinese baby girl. Coming from another race, in early infancy (usually within the first month) such a child could be regarded as having had no previous social existence. It started its effective life as a member of Malay society, and as the daughter of its purchasers. Although their Chinese origin might be made the basis of jibes later on, in general such children were treated as full children of their adoptive parents, and because of their fair skins might be expected to make good marriages. Because they were girls there were no complications about direct claims for political office, but informants also opined that their sons would not be chosen for office. Where property is concerned, a bought child should succeed to her share of both *pusaka* and other property.

The youngest people adopted in this way in the villages I studied were in their middle teens. It might be suggested that the reason for the decline of this practice was that Chinese no longer wish to sell their daughters, but it still occurs elsewhere in Malaya. I suggest that recent changes have increased the social distance between the two races in Jelebu, so that there is no longer the type of contact between the groups which would allow such transactions to take place.

Informal adoption, the rearing of a child by someone other than its real parents, without changing its jural status, is common. If a couple's children are all adult they will ask for one of their daughter's children to raise. This is especially common when a daughter has left the village with a wage-earning husband, and is acceptable to the child's parents as a form of economic aid, for many of them are hard pressed to raise large families on low wages.

Similarly, if a woman is barren she will ask for one of her sister's offspring. At one end of the scale I have a case where a sister almost completely replaced the mother, to such an extent that she arranged and carried out her adopted daughter's wedding, and had reared her completely since she was a small baby. Here only legal formality, an introduction of modern administration, and the knowledge that she had a 'real' mother (knowledge which seemed to mean very little emotionally), were all that differentiated the relationship from the actual mother-daughter tie. At the other end of the scale this kind of adoption may merely mean a temporary change of residence, the rights and responsibilities of parenthood still lying clearly with the real parents, to whom the child sooner or later returns.

MARRIAGE

Marriages are the main ceremonial and festive occasions of village life. The traditional season for weddings follows the harvest, especially when the lunar calendar allows a few weeks' interval before the start of the unlucky and inconvenient fasting month. This season is still a time of gaiety as one feast follows another, but modern economic changes have made for some move away from traditional timing. There is no slack period in an economy based on the daily tapping of rubber, except the rainy season, which is a time of hardship. Also, with so many young men in the Security Forces and other employment, factors such as the ability of the groom to get leave play an important part.

Marriages are arranged. There are no opportunities for social intercourse between young men and women in the villages. A daughter is expected to marry the man chosen for her. It is the height of immodesty for a girl to have any desires in this matter at all. A girl should not be married against her will, indeed, at the ceremony she must signify her consent before witnesses. But this consent shows passive acceptance rather than positive approval, and varying degrees of coercion may be used to obtain it. Even so, although I heard of several girls who were less than enthusiastic about the choice made for them, I never attended a wedding where the bride made a fuss about consenting when the time came.

A man has more freedom of choice. Should he resist his parents' first suggestion they will make another. He is also allowed to indicate to his family someone whom he would like them to ask for, and they should attempt to foresee his wishes if these become apparent in any way. But few youths avail themselves of this limited opportunity for choice; they restrict themselves to trying to find out something about, or at least to look at, the girl whom their parents suggest.

In arranging marriages the preference is for someone near. Cross-cousins are regarded as the nearest possible, and there are many marriages between them (especially of mother's–brother's daughter with father's–sister's son). This preference is not explicitly institutionalized. There is, for example, no terminological recognition of the relationship, nor special avoidances, nor will informants say that one should marry one's mother's–brother's daughter, although, if asked, they will agree that it is good. The nearness sought is rather social than purely genealogical, and the nature of relations between the parents might lead to a cross-cousin being passed over in favour of remoter kin, or even an unrelated person. In any case, in village society, if a candidate for *menantu* (child-in-law) is otherwise suitable, it is normally possible to find some connection to prove that he or she is 'not a stranger'.

However remote the connection may appear, there will be one, and one that is important in the concrete circumstances. This means that there is always one person, at least, strategically placed with a connection to both sides of the marriage. This can be clearest when the father of the bride is mother's brother to the groom, and especially so when the marriages form an exchange pattern over time, sons-in-law being drawn from the same group as the bride's father, while sons go as *menantu* to that group (*ikat sambar*).

The reason most often given for 'marrying near' is that the parents' property should not be enjoyed by a stranger when they die. But another reason is the sharing of poverty. When a father is poor, and his daughter consequently a poor match, it is common for him to put pressure on one of his kin to marry her. Indeed, people speak as if he had the right to 'take' one of his *anakbuah* in this way.

It is also thought to make for easier personal relations between the groom and the other occupants of the house to which he will transfer on marriage, if he is not a complete stranger.

Finally there is the notion that the very giving of one's son to another as *menantu* in itself constitutes a prestation. Female kin of the groom who accompany him at his wedding often remark, in the bandying of jokes and threats which accompanies the ceremony, that the bride's people have taken their child, and if he is not properly treated they will take him back. Partly it is a question of the transfer of his presence and earning capacity, but the concept of debts to one's children, especially marrying a daughter, is important.

If the marriage of a girl is delayed even slightly beyond the normal village marrying age (*c.* 14–16 years), gossip quickly points to the meanness of her parents who are trying to delay the expense, to their snobbish choosiness which leads them to refuse good offers from eligible young men, or to their avarice in insisting on too large a contribution to wedding expenses from the suitors, which failings, they say, will lead to the girl being left an 'old maid'. Also there will be malicious gossip and comment about the morals and ultimate fate of the girl if she is not soon properly settled with a husband. Marriage solves this problem; when fathers relax after the turmoil of a wedding they often express their relief that they have paid their debt. Providing the groom allows the debt to be paid, and so the kin of the new groom have conferred a benefit on his affines. The feeling that it is better to help one's own before helping strangers is another reason for 'marrying near'.

When informal discussion and inquiry have ascertained that a girl is suitable, and that suitors are likely to be welcome, a few women of the youth's kin go and make the first overture. If this is successful a date is fixed for the formal betrothal ceremony, at which an agreement is made, and tokens (rings) exchanged. It is the matrilineal elders, ideally the *ibubapa*, who conduct the proceedings. The whole tone of the ceremony stresses that one kin group are giving a member and another receiving him.

Informants said that a real wedding takes three days, but all the many weddings I saw, save one, were carried out in a night and a day. This is possible because nowadays many of the traditionally integral parts of the ceremony are only carried out in token, or not at all.

The ceremony falls into two parts, the religious ceremony (*kahwin ugama*) and the *adat* marriage. Although the religious ceremony may be carried out some time before it is convenient to hold the elaborate and costly *adat* ceremony, they are usually carried out consecutively.

On the appointed evening the groom appears at the bride's house accompanied by a few kin and a group of friends, who may be no kin at all and have the task of keeping him company. A relatively small feast will be in progress, and while the women and some of the men prepare for the bigger celebrations next day, the other men recite the *Maulud Nabi*. The actual wedding is given no prominence. The groom and the bride's father (or his representative as *wali* guardian) make the standardized verbal agreement in the presence of two witnesses and a few onlookers, while most of the people in the house carry on with their work or sit around and chat. Before the wedding the rings given as betrothal tokens are returned, and the 'marriage gold' ($24.00 for a maiden and $12.00 for a *janda* (divorcee or widow)) is paid.

The religious ceremony is all that is necessary and appropriate at the marriage of a *janda*, but for a maiden there remain the *adat* ceremonies before marital relations may commence.

That night or early the next morning the groom returns to his own house. The following day there are feasts at both houses. That at the groom's house is for the people who 'send' him; after this feast, at a time previously fixed, or on receiving a message from the bride's house, the groom leaves with a large party which gathers near the bride's home for a ceremonial entry. The bride's party meanwhile feast their guests and kin, and prepare to receive the groom.

Each party should have drums and men who know the chant, *zikir rebana*. The groom is hoisted on to the shoulders of relatives and friends, and, shaded by his umbrella, is slowly carried to the bride's house. A similar group bearing the bride (or in some places a little girl who represents her), comes out to meet them. Exchanging their respective burdens all proceed to the house. One other important item which the groom's party carry is his bag, the symbol that he is moving to a new home; a new suitcase carrying his clothes, a collection on which much money and thought will have been spent so that he will not feel *malu* before his new affines. On arrival the bag is taken from the groom's party and carried into the bridal chamber.

After some token resistance and a bribe the groom with the

female members of his party are led into the central (female/family) portion of the house. His party are now fed.

The *adat* ritual which follows has two important parts, *bersanding* and *mandi sampat*.

For the *bersanding* the couple are seated on an elaborate raised throne so that they may be seen by all kin and guests. While so seated they receive obeisance from about three members of each kin-group. One would expect a clear rule as to which categories of kin, and how many, should recognize the wedding in this way. What strikes the observer is the casualness with which the actual ritual is carried out, expecially in contrast to the careful material preparation. The attitude is *jangan ta'ada*, anything will do. A wedding is largely judged by the preparation of the house, the dress of the couple, the food, the smoothness of the catering arrangements and general absence of confusion.

Bersanding is common to all Malay weddings, *mandi sampat* is no longer widely practised outside Negri Sembilan. The couple are led from the house to a bamboo erection like the frame of a tent, and stand side by side within it while before them are placed on a tray, two candles, two coconuts (cut so that they will split if knocked over), some thread and materials for marking the forehead in blessing. The attendants of the couple (either kinswomen or professionals who also hire out the dresses for the weddings where they officiate) tie the couple together with the thread, light the candles, and then join the posts of the bamboo structure with fronds of palm leaves to enclose the couple.

The couple are now blessed by the kin of both parties. As with the *bersanding*, the attitude here too is concern that there be enough people to perform the blessing, rather than that particular categories of kin be represented.

After the blessing the attendants engage in some horseplay, pushing each other so that the fronds and cotton are broken, the candles extinguished, and the coconuts roll over, if possible with one rolling uphill and the other down. The couple are carried to the well or stream and bathe together. The ceremony is now complete.

On the following day the couple go with a group of the bride's relatives to the house of the groom. The procedure on this visit (*menyembah*) is very similar to that at the *bersanding* save that the celebration is smaller. That night should be spent at the groom's

house, after which the couple return to the bride's home to begin
a series of visits to their kin, especially hers.

These visits are formal, and, as the newly married couple travel
with a small party, they involve some expense for the people
they visit. Also the couple bring gifts of cakes which must be
reciprocated with money. It is fully in keeping with modern
attitudes that relatives commonly gather in one house to meet
the couple together, so lessening the number of feasts.

The parents of the bride and groom, who may not accompany
them during the ceremonies or at any of these visits, have to meet
each other through an exchange of visits known as *berbisan*.

Compared with the ritual outside Negri Sembilan, that of a
Jelebu wedding is remarkable for its relatively un-Muslim
character. The slight stress on the religious ceremony is especially
atypical. Elsewhere in Malaya this ceremony requires the presence
of religious dignitaries, such as the *imam* or *kadi*, and a marriage
sermon which it is the duty of one of these men to read. The contract is also made the focus of attention at a feast, and is not just
one more activity going on amidst the turmoil of feast preparations. In Jelebu religious dignitaries attend weddings on the same
terms as everyone else, because it is appropriate for them to come
on grounds of kinskip, friendship, or the status of the families
involved. Conversely, under traditional arrangements precedence
is accorded *adat* chiefs in a way that is naturally not found elsewhere.

Probably at most weddings the participants feel themselves
more closely allied to either the bride or the groom. Even the
Anglican ceremony has a conventional expression of this with
guests of the bride and groom occupying different sides of the
aisle. In Negri Sembilan this is not an ephemeral grouping in the
context of the wedding, but an occasion where two corporate
groups are brought into relation. A cousin marriage in Negri
Sembilan can pose no problem for near kin about where their
primary duty lies. On the other hand, I have witnessed discussions
elsewhere in Malaya where the claims of the bride's and groom's
families have had to be very carefully weighed, and the reluctant
conclusion reached that one or the other had to be offended.

What is the role of the *orang semanda*, and especially of the
fathers of the couple in these ceremonies? The ceremony is pre-
ceded some weeks before by a meeting (*berkampong*). Here

arrangements are discussed and settled. The *orang semanda* must be invited for they are expected to bear the brunt of the work. Close neighbours should also be invited, for their help is expected too, and as neighbours they have the right to know what is going on near their homestead. But this is a formality. Neighbours are invited for the same reason that they attend, 'to show a good heart', not to help in planning and decisions. The *orang semanda* too must remember that the wedding is not their affair at all: because they are married to women of the group they have acquired the duty of working, but as long as their share of the feast is set aside for them they must follow whatever arrangements the *tempat semanda* see fit to make. Even the bride's father, apart from his role as guardian, *wali*, which he is in any case likely to delegate to someone else, should keep to the background as just another of the *orang semanda*, while leadership and decisions come from the male kin who have gathered for the meeting, and later for the ceremony.

This is the ideology of the situation under *adat*, and, particularly at a wedding, participants continually make comments on their role in it in keeping with this ideology, especially the *orang semanda* drawing attention to their inferior role in mock self depreciation. In practice, although the *orang semanda* play no ceremonial part they are likely to be very important in the direction of affairs, for they are the men on the spot.

Futhermore, it is the father who pays for the wedding, and has the major say in deciding how large expenses may be, and the nature of the expenses to be incurred. Wedding costs amount to at least several hundred dollars, and the bulk of this money the father finds himself. If a man's sons are in a position to help, say, if they are wage-earners with savings, they will do so, but this is not a source available to everyone. Also guests at a wedding make small gifts, which are listed with a view to repayment at some future feast of the donor. Many of the presents are cloth and decorated eggs, and these, while welcome, do not help defray cash expenses. As a rule the cash contributions are too small to meet expenses, in contrast to Kelantan (Rosemary Firth, 1943) where a profit is expected. In only one case did I learn of a man roughly recouping his monetary outlay in this way. Even then, he provided the feast item, a bull, and if he had had to buy it there would have been a deficit.

Finally, although male kin know that they are within their rights in matters affecting their sisters and their sisters' children, they also know that the houses, which are the kin-group base, are also the homes, and often the fruit of the labour, of the *orang semanda*, and since they, in turn, are *orang semanda* elsewhere, they can appreciate the feelings involved.

Whatever the theory of *adat*, and whatever the situation in the past, nowadays the rights of the *orang semanda* and the rights of the father of a child, are very important and real, although they have yet to find ideological expression of the same prestige as *adat;* in the meantime the villagers adjust their respective claims in accordance with their ideals of reasonableness and avoiding fuss.

Divorce

Divorce is very common throughout Malay society, with divorces in any one year tending to be about half the number of registered marriages. Jelebu is no exception to this rule, as the accompanying Table 3 shows. I have argued (Swift, 1958) that the

TABLE 3.   Marriage and Divorce Statistics

	Marriages	Divorces	Revocations
1950	215	101	11
1951	216	134	12
1952	155	123	13
1953	165	85	3
1954	162	85	14
1955	157	66	7
1956	176	88	12
1957	197	102	11
1958	163	98	19
1959	172	99	14
1960	138	87	16

These figures, together with comparable statistics for the rest of the state, were supplied me through the kindness of Tuan Haji Anjang Saith, Head of the Department of Religious Affairs, Negri Sembilan, to whom I take this opportunity of expressing my grateful thanks.

divorce pattern in Jelebu differed from that prevailing elsewhere and attempted an explanation in terms of the consequences of matrilineal kinship organization. I maintained that marriage in

Jelebu was more stable than elsewhere, and that where divorce did occur the unions of those who had lost a former spouse through death or divorce were particularly fragile. Now that I am in possession of the broad figures for the District and the State I can no longer maintain this proposition in its entirety, although there is still no reason to abandon the second point. The difficulty which I now face is that neither my own village census (Table 2) nor my impressions of the District, conform to this picture of very fragile marriage. There are in any case considerable statistical difficulties in comparing my data with the official figures. These latter give no information about the duration of the marriage dissolved by a divorce, nor any guide as to the number of previous marriages of the divorcers. To some extent the high figures are due to the same people occurring over and over again; I also expect new marriages to be less stable than those of the now middle-aged.

It follows that the following discussion of divorce is not 'typical' of Jelebu; I nevertheless feel it is worthwhile presenting as an empirical example of the way in which matrilineal kinship organization does bear on the frequency of divorce. The connection between kinship and divorce is a question that has often been raised. For the Hopi Eggan has suggested a correlation between unilineal kinship, especially matrilineal kinship, and divorce, in a discussion which raises many points of comparison with matrilineal Jelebu (Eggan, 1949). Gluckman, contrasting the Lozi and the Zulu, stated a number of interesting hypotheses concerning marriage stability, some of which have been fruitfully applied by Djamour (1959) to the problem of Malay divorce. As my admittedly inadequate material bears directly on the questions she has raised I venture to present it, while hoping that someone, equipped with the resources which a full sample survey dealing with Malay divorce would require, will soon be attracted to the problem.

THE LEGAL SYSTEM

In any society the frequency of divorce must be partly determined by the ease with which one may be obtained. As elsewhere in Malaya, Malay divorce and marriage in Negri Sembilan are bound by Muslim law. Under this law a husband may obtain divorce at will simply by informing his wife that he divorces her.

This is subject only to the modern requirement that the divorce be registered with the *Kadi* (fee $5.00). For a wife divorce on her own initiative would appear so difficult that she has no alternative but to tolerate a distasteful marriage. In fact a woman can easily drive her husband to divorce her out of exasperation. Short of this a woman desiring a divorce is aided by the notion that a man should be ashamed to refuse a divorce to a woman who no longer wants him: 'there are plenty of other women'.

Shame also helps deter a man from leaving his wife 'hanging' (*gantong ta'bertali*), married but not receiving any maintenance from him, unable to remarry while he can readily take another wife. This behaviour is only tolerated when the husband is felt to have been severely provoked, and even then he should just divorce her and forget her. It is demeaning to allow oneself to be upset by a woman's behaviour.

In summary, then, divorce is readily obtainable by either spouse.

VALUE-ATTITUDES TOWARDS DIVORCE

Divorce carries no stigma, and there is no moral prestige gained by putting up with a marriage that has become unsatisfactory. Although there may be in certain circumstances strong pressures against divorce, in general it is just as normal as marriage. People speak of divorce as though it were an ever-present possibility within any marriage. In justifying the exclusion of the *orang semanda* from *perut* affairs the expression 'he is not fixed here' is often used, even if the man in question is old and has been only married to the one woman throughout his career. The phrase implies that the *orang semanda* is likely, at any time, to divorce his wife and return to his matrilineal kin, 'his place'.

Divorce, or its likelihood, looms large in village gossip, and the villagers' amused attitude shows that there is not the slightest condemnation felt towards divorce as long as the parting is managed without unseemly discord and emotion. If anything it is the man who divorces his wife rather than tolerate any 'fuss' from her or her kin who performs a laudable act.

Legally, and in value-attitudes, the situation is similar to that elsewhere in Malay society, and yet I did not find divorce resulting from the domestic discord I observed, while I did find people who threatened to divorce being restrained from doing so by a number of factors which I will now describe.

Outside Negri Sembilan Malay kinship is bilateral (cognatic) with bias towards the father's kin in some contexts and towards the mother's in others. So, instead of the corporate groupings of clan and subclan, there are only a series of personal kin-groupings, the same only for children of the same father and mother. I believe this contrast in kinship organization has important implications for the understanding of Jelebu divorce. In amplification of this it is necessary to discuss the different meaning a divorce will have for the individuals affected in differing circumstances.

THE IMPLICATIONS OF DIVORCE

Two distinctions are necessary for this analysis. First, separate the 'reactions of the kin-group' to a divorce, and the 'practical considerations' relevant to an individual decision whether to divorce or not. Secondly, two phases in the development of a marriage must be distinguished. The first is the 'adjustment period' which begins at the wedding and continues until the couple are accepted as fully adult members of the community. The terminal point is necessarily subjective for it reflects the judgement of the villagers on the conduct of the young couple. As an objective criterion some reliance may be placed on the birth of the first child and the move of the couple into their own house. Even then, however, it is still possible to hear a young man, who has fulfilled these qualifications, dismissed as *akal belum sampai lagi* (not yet acquired intelligence). The second phase is full adulthood.

(1) *The adjustment period*

All Malay youths recognize the necessity of marriage, and may even welcome it as a step towards full adulthood. Nevertheless there are disadvantages which weigh heavily with a young man. He must accept the authority of his *mentua* (parent-in-law) and of the *tempat semanda*. This may well be an unpleasant contrast with his spoiled status in his mother's house and his freedom with the peer-group. A preference for arranging near marriages helps to make this adjustment less irksome than it might otherwise be, but even in a 'near' marriage a youth may not have been on terms of close friendship with his new affines. In the reminiscences of old men, the complaints of middle-aged and young married men, and the anticipations of youths about to be married, trouble with the *mentua* and affines looms large.

The groom has to assume responsibility for the support of his wife, and this too will be an unpleasant contrast with his relative affluence before marriage.

Finally he will probably have to give up participating in the amusements of his friends in the peer-group, partly because 'playing about' is no longer fitting, and his *mentua* will not like it, and partly because he can no longer afford it. Moreover, even if he has married in a neighbouring village, it will be too far for him to mix with his former friends as freely as before, while the youth of the new village are, at best, remote in their attitude towards him.

The bride has first of all the problem of getting used to her husband (I find myself here taking over the judgement of the Malay which sees this as a problem for a bride but not a groom). As I have said, her consent to the marriage is little more than a formality. Even if the groom is a cousin she will not have seen much of him since they were small children, and will probably know little more of her husband than the praises of the people who want her to accept her lot cheerfully. As a young man in a Muslim society there were many obstacles to my studying the reactions of new brides closely. The only women whom I could question were too far from their own marriages to give 'honest' replies. That is to say, they were more concerned with the question of marrying their daughters than in their own reactions as new brides. I heard several accounts of girls who refused to sleep with their husbands, or refused to speak, or even to look at them, for some time after the wedding. I have heard my young friends (as scared and embarrassed as girls) earnestly discussing the use of magic oil (*minyak sayang*) to make their wives accept them when first married, and how to coax them. On the other hand, none of the girls that I knew of who got married seemed to show any extreme reactions. The answers of older women and male informants to questions about a girl's reaction to an arranged marriage suggest that adjustment difficulties are likely. 'Of course she will like him' was the most frequent reply; and further questions would elicit, 'No one wants to make their own child unhappy, but what does a young girl know about these things?'

Not only must she adjust to her husband and the sexual aspects of her new role, but a girl also has to work harder after marriage.

Although a daughter plays an important part in the work of the household, much more so than her brother, she will not usually have to work very hard, and she is helping her mother without being definitely responsible for specific tasks. She will usually have some choice about what she wants to do. Above all it is not proper that she work in the ricefields. After marriage, although she is still living with her mother, and although they are operating a joint household, the responsibility of attending to her husband's domestic needs is definitely hers, and more generally, she will bear a fuller share of the household domestic work than she did before marriage.

The disadvantages of marriage for both the young bride and groom could easily be avoided by divorce. The young man can revert to the status of *budak-budak kampong* (lads of the village) returning to his mother's house, and mixing with his former friends (until they in turn marry) on much the same terms as before. A girl too automatically reverts to being a dependant of her father, and, particularly before the birth of her first child, there will be little difference in status between her and her unmarried sisters.

It would therefore be reasonable to expect a high frequency of divorce during this adjustment period; but it is now that the influence of the kin-group becomes important.

One aspect of Malay indulgence towards the young is that they are regarded as too irresponsible to be expected, or allowed, to manage their own affairs when an issue of any importance is involved. Attitudes to the young are far from stern, but a definite authority attaches to age and seniority, and this will be brought to bear if it seems likely that a divorce will result from the 'foolishness' of the young. A particular marriage is arranged because it seems, on objective considerations, the most advantageous possible. The principals' temporary dislike of the situation is not seen as sufficient reason for reappraising the decision.

When a young man is contemplating divorce a common first step is for him to 'run' to his own house, usually without pronouncing even the first *talak*.[1] As he has strong ties there it will not seem strange if he says that he has arrangements to make there or proffers some other excuse. Often it is only after some days that his wife's family begin to feel concern about his failure

---

[1] *Talak,* the divorce formula. See Djamour (1959, 110ff.) for a discussion of this and other aspects of divorce law and procedure.

to return. Similarly his own family may only realize after a few days, and from his evasive replies to questions about when he intends to return to his wife, that all is not well with the *tempat semanda*. In other cases the 'running' may well have a more explosive prelude, an open quarrel with his wife or one of her kin.

Whatever the course taken, as soon as the relatives realize that a divorce may occur they begin informal discussions, while each attempts to get their own member to accept reconciliation.

To the man the advantages of this woman as against any other will be stressed. In this society prolonged bachelorhood is most unusual, and the young man will know that if it is not this wife, with this *mentua* and this *tempat semanda*, it will soon have to be another. It is also felt to be desirable that a youth should have married and left if a married sister is still living in the parental home, and young informants have remarked to me that they felt awkward with their brother-in-law in this situation.

The wife's kin too will try and persuade her to make the conciliatory visit 'inviting back'. A proper 'inviting back' after an acknowledged breach requires that she be accompanied by kin, and carry the betel equipment which is such an important part of Malay etiquette. This visit places her and her kin in the position of asking the man to return, and this is essential, regardless of which party may have been at fault in the initial difference (or indeed, even if the husband is the party mainly desirous of reconciliation—his pride will nevertheless require it). The remarks people make on such occasions, and general discussions of the position of *janda* in the village, show a belief that it is more difficult for a woman to find another husband than a man another wife. I see no foundation for this, but the argument is used to make a girl who does not like her husband tolerate him. The pressure put on the young spouses can take many forms. The family may gently agree, but nevertheless ask him or her to try again for their sakes. They may try to persuade them that things are not as bad as they seem and will soon improve. Outright anger, and for girls slapping and pinching and the threat that if she divorce this husband she will be given to an old man next time may also be used. Such suasion was effective in most of the cases which came to my attention.

The fact that so much pressure is brought to bear on young people in danger of divorce is to be explained by the role of group representative played by every young spouse. In unilineal kinship organization marriage has a group relations significance which it cannot have in a bilateral system. The corporate kinship group, with definite single membership, gives sole loyalty and identification, in sharp contrast to the complex web of ties which surrounds each individual in a bilateral system. Elsewhere in Malaya divorce is likely to lead to bad relations between the immediate kin of the former spouses, but it does not set in opposition two of the major groupings of the society.[1] The character of marriage as a relation between groups is emphasized by the pattern of preferential marriage, which means that any particular marriage is only one of a series of relationships binding two groups. Accordingly it is desirable to avoid divorce for fear of ramifying bad relations which will endanger the stability of the other marriages.

This stress on the relation between two groups can be seen throughout the wedding ceremonials, save in the religious ceremony which is the least emphasized element. The betrothal, at which the subclan chiefs or other senior males agree to the wedding and the date before witnesses, implies the consent, at least tacit, of all the group. Therefore they share in the obligation to see that the agreement is properly fulfilled. This means not only that the wedding should take place, but that a satisfactory marriage should result. In one case her kin forced a *janda*, who had rejected her husband soon after marrying him with her free consent, to 'invite him back', and told her she would have to wait for a decent interval before the man divorced her, and must behave herself in the meantime. Had she not done so the groom's kin were threatening to demand twice the marriage gold in compensation, and a *timbang salah* feast. Their concern is largely to be explained by the respected status and clan office of the groom who had found himself placed in a humiliating situation. Nowadays, if the offending group do not care whether they are on good terms with the groom's kin or not, there are no sanctions to make them pay compensation, but formerly even bad relations arising from marital disputes were politically sanctioned.

Informants asserted that in the past it was essential for all

---

[1] In a bilateral system the multiple loyalties and cross-cutting of kin ties within a narrow social field must serve to limit the harmful effects on social integration of divorce, and so make a high divorce rate more tolerable.

disputes within a group to be settled before a wedding took place, so that everyone might participate, and so be committed to the social relationships created by the ceremony. Men who are on bad terms with some of their kin-group sometimes announce that they are going to *tahan* a wedding, i.e. prevent its taking place. No one denies their *adat* prerogative to do this, but if good relations cannot be restored the ceremony is still carried out. Even so, unity is still the ideal, and those immediately concerned with a ceremony endeavour to reconcile their own differences and those of others in the group. Nowadays an unsettled quarrel within the *perut* does not mean that a wedding cannot take place, but it is felt to be 'not as good' as one carried out with the cooperation of all kin. There is an expectation that an attempt at reconciliation will be made; there is a moral judgement that people should be particularly prepared on such occasions to settle differences which in any case ought not to exist, but there is no longer any fear that failure to achieve unity will prevent the ceremony.

I am arguing that the group character of marriage, and the authority which elders can exercise over the young, combine to prevent divorce during a particularly unstable phase of the marriage.

(2) *The adult phase of a marriage*

For an adult considering divorce the importance of the influence of group pressure and practical interest is reversed. The adult is left to manage his own affairs without any great pressure from the kin-group (although he may well rely heavily on advice from one or more members of it). Even should there be any desire to intervene an adult is not subject to control by his elders in the same way as a newly married couple. Unless there are complicating factors, such as a dispute over the division of joint property, a husband-wife quarrel and divorce will not usually lead to general bad relations between their respective kin.

In the first place it is recognized that the group cannot really be held responsible for the actions of its adult members in the same way that it is for an adolescent member. Secondly, divorce after a marriage has been established for some years does not constitute a breach of the agreement between the groups as does divorce when a marriage has hardly started. Finally, if two adults decide to divorce it cannot be dismissed as a temporary reaction to a change in status to which the couple will become reconciled if they are restrained from an initial resolve to divorce.

But if kin-group pressure is weaker the pull of practical interests is much stronger on a husband and wife who have been married for some considerable time.

Most men build houses on their wives' homestead, and after divorce these houses become the property of the wife. This may well represent a large loss. A newly married man's first house, if he is not still living with his *mentua*, will probably be a mere bamboo shack, representing the investment of little more than labour.

The older man is differently placed too with regard to returning to his matrilineal kin. For the young newly married man, it is simply a question of reverting to the status of unmarried son in his mother's house. For an older man, even if his parents are still alive and able to accept him, this position is not satisfactory to a man who has been *tuan rumah*, master in his own house. What is more, for many men returning home means going to live in a sister's house, a household headed by a brother-in-law. A man has inalienable rights in ancestral property, the use and title to which is vested in his sisters, and their house is the proper place for him to go on divorce, or at the death of his wife. Even so, he is likely to find that his prolonged residence there is regarded as an imposition rather than the enjoyment of a legitimate privilege. The relations between a woman's husband and her brother are a point of structural tension, and friction is probable if they occupy the same house. Even sisters, finding their work increased and their domestic arrangements upset, may wish that their brother would marry again and move out. Some men whose mothers have died, and who have no sisters with whom they might stay, are faced with the fact that they would be homeless if divorced, for nowadays more remote kin would not welcome a long-term lodger, and most men would be too *malu* to try.

A man who divorces his wife loses his children. They will stay with their mother, and the most a man can expect is that they will come and stay with him for a few days occasionally. Even this may be difficult. Some wives resent their husband's children by a former marriage, and the children themselves, if he left them while they were still young, may refuse to stay with their father, for they are not used to him, and cry to return to their mother.

He is still their father; his status as *wali* of his daughter cannot be taken away from him. He has the right of access to his children, but since divorce usually implies bad feeling, and since his former wife will probably have another husband, this right is probably difficult to exercise, especially since ideas of propriety condemn any contact between a man and his *janda*, so much so that I have heard a man criticized for walking in front of his former wife's house when there was a detour available. Children are recognized by the villagers as a powerful influence restraining a man from divorce.

For a woman the consequences of divorce may be even more serious. Should her father be able to support her he will do so. Indeed I have known two cases where the daughters of wealthy peasants, after a disappointing first marriage, announced that they were never going to marry again, and whose parents seemed prepared to accept this decision. But for most women, especially those left with young children to support, the prospect is one of economic hardship. Occasionally a woman may get some assistance from her former spouse for the maintenance of their children. This may be obtained through the influence of the Social Welfare Department or of the *Kadi*; here the payments are voluntary. Or she might get a Court Order, in which case the father will be forced to pay. This is common practice in large towns such as Singapore, but the village Malay is not familiar with Court procedure for any save land cases. Also it is a step which places him in a bad light in village opinion, for outsiders should not be brought into village affairs, where disputes should be settled by 'agreement', *muafakat*. Only one case of this kind came to my attention, and here I feel the anger of the girl's father was a major factor. Continual struggle was necessary to get the money. When the former husband had been summoned for non-payment several times the girl's father gave up trying, for other villagers criticized him for causing trouble to his former son-in-law's parents who had to pay to keep their son out of gaol, and also for making an unbecoming fuss.

People often say that they would rather do without money from the father, for they prefer his claim to the child to lapse, and while he continues to support the child his claims cannot be denied.

Living very frugally a woman can probably manage with the

rice land, and perhaps the little rubber and fruit, that she owns. She will become a familiar sight around the village collecting wild vegetables, and catching the small fish of the drains and rice-fields which most people do not ordinarily bother about. Goods normally bought, such as salt, peppers and oil, she can obtain only with difficulty, let alone such things as clothes and cigarettes.

This economic difficulty arises because the main source of cash for the purchase of consumption goods is rubber tapping and in Jelebu it is uncommon for women to undertake this sort of work. Nor do many of the women own rubber land from which they might derive an income. Inheritance shares tend to be equal, regardless of the sex of the child, but rubber is felt more appropriate to the needs of a man, who will have the responsibility of finding money for his family, while a woman should possess the necessary ricefield and homestead. I have known economically hard-pressed *janda* take up rubber tapping for a while. They do not tap full lots, such as a man works, but only small patches of poor quality trees found on the village outskirts. But they prefer to struggle along without such work. Although rubber tapping is not women's work the Malay attitude to the division of labour by sexes is practical, and a woman who tried to make ends meet in this way would not be criticized. What deters the women is the thought that they are making their poverty apparent for all to see.

It would be possible to continue with more illustrations of the practical difficulties which confront a divorced person; for example, the way in which a woman without a husband finds it difficult to attend ceremonies outside the village, and so is cut off from one of the most enjoyed excitements in a rather confined life. But besides the more calculable practical profit and loss, elements such as affection and inertia provide powerful support for a marriage which can survive the adjustment period and has lasted for some time.

For the adult kin-group interest is directed not so much towards preserving a marriage, but rather to finding a new spouse after divorce; indeed, should a man complain about his wife the advice that he will get will probably be to divorce rather than put up with it, or to keep quiet and not demean himself talking about his private affairs. Recently bereaved or divorced spouses, even if they feel no great hurry to marry again are subject to continual advice, persuasion and propositions until they relent. Pressure is particularly strong on women. The economic difficulties of a *janda* have already been mentioned. But a *janda* is also considered to be in great moral danger without a man to look after her. Conduct that in a married woman would not be noticed will in her case be censured and seen as evidence of worse. It could almost be said that the word *janda* is worth a snigger in itself. Should they delay in finding her a new spouse a *janda*'s male kin and affines (sister's husbands) will be criticized, on the one hand for not finding her a man to provide for her, but also for not guarding the reputation of the kin-group and the village properly.

A wifeless man is more independent than a *janda*, but he too will face attempts to match him off. As a strong inducement he has his own discomfort with no proper place to live, and no-one to provide domestic services for him. His matrilineal kin will probably not relish his prolonged residence with them, and in any case, feel a responsibility to see him settled once more. He is also subject to the wiles of those who see him as a suitable match for a *janda* under their care.

Such subsequent marriages are not very durable. Neither the influence of the kin-group (for they take little interest in the marital affairs of adults) nor the practical interests which grow up with a marriage (for they are too new) can exert a binding influence. In these later marriages the contractual element is even more explicit; the parties come together only as individuals seeking mutual gain from the division of labour by sex, and only to a limited extent are they representatives of their kin, unlike the young couple joined in a first marriage. In such circumstances, if either party is dissatisfied the logical thing is to divorce and try again, and that is what people often do.

The simplicity and cheapness of subsequent marriages is a factor disposing people to regard them casually. A simple meal for a few guests; a marriage gold payment of only $12.00, and only the plain religious ceremony.

I have been arguing that unilineal kinship organization, which is found in Negri Sembilan society, and still differentiates it from other Malay society, works for marriage stability, through the collective involvement of the group in the early phase of a marriage, when it would seem a particularly fragile tie. Members of the descent group have the opportunity and incentive to restrain younger kinsfolk from divorce during the adjustment period. As an individual acquires adult status this influence weakens, but at the same time the stability of the marriage can increasingly depend on a complex of practical interests which develops within it.

I do not argue that matrilineal kinship organization necessarily tends to lessen the frequency of divorce; on the contrary, divorce, by ejecting the non-member (the *orang semanda*) and bringing back male members married elsewhere, would seem to favour integration of the kin-groups, subject only to the provision that, given exogamy, some arrangements must be made for recruitment. Also, although the descent group system means control of the young in the interests of group relations, it also means that a man is controlled within his own (wife's) house. This latter feature of the system must be expected to make for tension between a man and his wife's kin, which can lead to his divorcing her. Indeed, this effect can still be seen to some extent, and informants' reminiscences lead me to believe that it was once more pronounced. In terms of our analysis these strains will develop during the adult phase of a marriage when a man will expect independence to manage his own affairs. In the process of its decline *adat* has weakened more with regard to husband–wife relations than it has with regard to the authority of age.

I believe that were the information available it would be possible to distinguish three phases: (i) the traditional system in which a powerful *adat*, and the political sanctioning of the *orang semanda – tempat semanda* relationship, made for frequent divorce. (ii) An interim stage, when the most powerful pressures of *adat* on the nuclear family have weakened, but the group relations character of the marriage tie is still strong enough for the group to resist divorce during the adjustment period, (iii) and finally, a bilateral family organization, with divorce as frequent as elsewhere in Malay society.

The figures for the District as a whole suggest that most of Jelebu has already reached this final stage. Even within the group of villages which I studied, where I found marriage more stable than the Registration figures would suggest, signs of a trend towards more frequent divorce could be seen, concentrated mainly in the younger generation.

Wage labour takes a man away from the village, and he may

well marry a woman in the place where he is working, or a
relative of one of his fellow workers. Although such a wedding
may be given the same ceremonial start as a wedding between
two Jelebu kin-groups, it will not create a firm tie because of the
distance involved, and also because it is probably the only tie
between the groups.

Although it is admittedly highly subjective, I maintain that the
rate of decline of kinship organization is not the same in all groups.
Some *perut* give an impression of greater solidarity and concern
for traditional values, while others appear to be only nominal
corporate groups. With these latter marriage cannot have the
same effect in creating group relations, nor can the same pressures
restrain young couples from divorce. I also formed a strong impression that where a group could not maintain its solidarity,
as shown in intra-group friendliness and cooperation, its members
were 'useless' also in terms of the other values of the society.
Some families seemed to have a higher proportion of lazy, un-
reliable or even dishonest people, who not only ignore obligations
according to *adat* but flout the values still valid.

A distinction might be made between groups leaving *adat*
'positively' and those doing so 'negatively'. In the first type the
group may have committed some offence it is not prepared to
repair, or a quarrel with the clan chief may have led to their being
ignored in ceremonial and succession to office. Even so, the group
still maintains its internal solidarity, members still cooperate and
support each other, and the group is still a collectivity in a real
sense. Where the people have left the *adat* negatively, it represents
a failure to conform to any rules which are not strongly sanctioned.
There is no decision to flout or ignore *adat*, it simply dies because
no one is interested in it. Examples here would be groups prepared to lose their *pusaka* simply because no member thought
office worth the trouble. Such people also tend to have bad
relations in the nuclear family, to be poor participants in village
cooperation, bad debtors and inferior workers. If they are more
prone to divorce there is no need to invoke unilineal kinship for
an explanation; rather we must look at their mildly deviant
character. Lest these ideas seem too loose for scientific argument
I should like to add that by using them I have been able to predict some divorces, and have seen my predictions fulfilled.

Working outside the village not only makes for marriage

between socially distant individuals; it also effectively removes the young from the control of their elders. If a young couple quarrel in Police or Army quarters miles from home, and the husband either sends his wife back to her village, or allows her to return, it is the equivalent to a young man 'running' home from his wife's village. The next stage would normally be for the kin to start to attempt a reconciliation. When the young man is working far away, however, there is little they can do. He can divorce his wife by post, or marry another woman locally while his wife is away; if his kin are angry, or his wife's kin are threatening him, he can refuse to come home on leave, or, if he returns and is met with anger, simply go off again.

Finally, working away from the village implies exposure to different values, and a tendency to accept the fact that the values of fellow workers, also Malays, but from other areas, are as valid as one's own. Other Malays tend to see *adat perpateh* as an odd deviation from the 'normal' Malay pattern. I believe that Negri Sembilan Malays tend to accommodate to majority cultural standards when working away from the village, especially within the community atmosphere of Police Barracks and Army Camp, and since it is in the area of kinship behaviour that the difference between Negri Sembilan and the rest is most marked, it is here that we may expect to see this accommodation most evident.

CHAPTER X

Family and Domestic Groups (2)

WIDER GROUPINGS

Every family is connected closely in everyday affairs with a small group of surrounding households. These are the families of the near female kin (sisters and cousins, mother and mother's sisters) of the wife/mother. The primary foundation of this grouping is the relationships formed within the wife's family of orientation. The persistence of these ties is aided by close proximity of residence, for the houses will normally be located on a single piece of land transmitted in the female line, and divided in each generation. A further source of strength for this grouping lies in its institutionalization. Not only are the women accustomed to cooperate, like it, and find it convenient because they live near each other, but they are expected to do so. Generally such a group is referred to as 'X's people' or 'X's brothers and sisters' using the name of a prominent member, sometimes it may even be referred to as a *perut*, although the primary meaning of this term is subclan in the sense of a named group led by an *ibubapa*. I will refer to this grouping as an extended family; as a domestic group it will include the women's husbands, and exclude their brothers, who are, however, members of the extended family as a kinship unit while their husbands are not. This group is not clearly bounded, for while an observer can clearly identify central or core members, at the edges of the group it may be hard to decide whether a particular family belong or not. It is this group of close kin which is the effective unit for most matters save election to office, and even then there may develop an informal rotation between the extended families of a subclan.

This is the group of women who will work together in all domestic activities which require cooperation or permit sociability. Where a woman lives some distance from her near relatives she is more likely to walk over and join them than to form new ties with her neighbours, despite the high valuation placed on neighbourliness.

Land shortage is tending to lessen the territorial unity of these matrilineal groups. Where a line has been very productive of daughters, and they have not left the village with wage-earning husbands, crowding has sometimes forced families to occupy new sites. Shortage of house sites has even led some groups to ignore the traditional categories of land use (though these are supported by the Government's issuing different types of title for different types of land). People can be found building houses in the rice-fields, moving from the usual hill slopes to the valley floor, but still keeping near their kin.

This process is aided by an increasing propensity to regard land as an economic good, freely to be bought and sold. Much of the land referred to as *tanah pusaka* is in fact held under ordinary title; although it is not bought and sold, is regarded as special, and will pass to daughters according to *adat* rules, the only sanction is the sentiment of the owners. When a woman dies without leaving daughters there is a feeling that her land should go to her sons rather than to more remote female kin. Informants saw this as natural and just, and replied to my questions about inheritance by nieces with 'that was before'. The only qualification would be that were the man not in need of land, and unable to use it, while there were near members of this *perut* who did and could, he should let the land go to them. Within the village the operation of the *adat* code depends on the villager's interpretation of it, and, should a case go to court, on the attitude of the *lembaga* who gives technical evidence, and the magistrate's understanding of a code which even Malays from other areas find unnatural, and the more educated people of Negri Sembilan oldfashioned.

The purchase of house sites is not yet common, although the increasing difficulty for some groups of finding suitable sites on their ancestral plots while neighbouring land stands idle, suggests that it soon must. Villagers are used to the idea of buying land which yields an income, but house sites have been scarce for a comparatively short time. Even now non-kin are allowed to use a vacant house-site, although the people 'squatting' (*tumpang*) dislike feeling dependent on someone else's good will.

In the village where I lived all sales of homestead land could be traced to two large lots which the owners had sold off in smaller parcels. In one case the land was *tanah pusaka*, but the line of inheritance had been reduced to one man, living with his wife some three miles away. He allowed quasi-kin (a *kadim* relationship) to buy half the land, but refused many subsequent offers for the remainder of the lot, saying that it was all he had left of his mother. It was continually pointed out to him that he had no need of the land while there were others who had. He had no other relatives within the village. His grandmother had come and *kadim* with a local family, and produced only one daughter, who in turn had produced only one son, the present owner. Even so, when he was finally persuaded to sell it was the adopted kin, those sharing the same *pusaka* through fictional kinship, who were the purchasers. This might appear as a transfer within the kinship group, recognizing the option of kin, but it was not so. The ties created two generations ago had almost completely lapsed, so that the younger members of the larger group were not even aware of them. Where this fictional kinship became important was in providing the seller with a justification for selling the land which was a souvenir of his mother.

The other piece of land has a more interesting history from the point of view of *adat*. The land, a piece of about three acres, had belonged to a woman who allowed her male cousin to use it. He had lived there partly because his wife's village was crowded, but also because, being a *lembaga*, he preferred to live on the land of his own kin where he would be independent of the *tempat semanda*. Through his position he was able to get the title of the land transferred to his wife through a process now obscure. In doing so he removed the land from the category of *tanah pusaka*. His only child was a daughter, and she proved barren. For this reason she was divorced by her husband, who left her very wealthy, by village standards, after the division of the joint property. At various times she sold pieces of this land for her maintenance, and for the pilgrimage to Mecca, retaining of the homestead plot only sufficient for the site of her own small house. In this way some of her kin were introduced into the village from the neighbouring one. But her selling of this land to her kin should not be regarded as an expression of an *adat* obligation. For one thing, she sold a large piece of the land to people of a completely different clan. Even the purchasers of her land from the next village, who were of the same subclan, were remote kin, and did not maintain close ties with her when they were neighbours. The next village is crowded, for the land rises steeply from the valley floor leaving only a narrow strip above the ricefields suitable for house building; these people first started building houses in the ricefields. Individuals forced to move will not go farther than is necessary, so that they can maintain their old relationships easily, and when one family has moved, others who have to go will prefer to follow the first migrants, rather than be totally isolated somewhere else. It is a matter of chance that in this case the supply of land and the demand came from the same kinship source.

Many men express a desire to purchase their own homestead land and build a house on it, rather than continue to live on their wives' *tanah pusaka*. Then, they say, the *tempat semanda* will not be able to interfere. Few of them do so, and in only one case have I clear evidence that trouble with the *tempat semanda* was the motive, although this feeling of freedom is an additional benefit accruing to the man who buys *kampong*.

Resettlement has entailed some distortion of residence patterns. Even where people have not been moved from their former villages, those living on the jungle fringe have been required to move into more accessible parts of the village. Some people have been able to find sites near relatives, while others have been forced to 'squat', with the owner's permission, on the land of non-kin. In late 1957 and 1958 the restrictions were gradually eased, and in February 1959 Negri Sembilan was declared a 'White Area'. There are now no restrictions on the residence of Malays and a return to the kinship pattern of dwelling is clearly visible. Adjustment cannot be immediate however. Moving a house, or building a new one, is not an everyday affair, and must await a favourable opportunity, and the accumulation of some cash resources.

The matrilineal extended family is almost the complete social milieu of the women and younger children of the group. Men are not so closely restricted. They entered the group only at marriage, and former ties persist. Indeed, as a man moves into a position of authority and responsibility with increasing age his ties with his kin may strengthen. A man also moves freely in the wider society. He goes to the town, the mosque, the coffee shop; there are many opportunities for social intercourse closed to women. To a limited extent, whether or not a man has close ties with his *biras* (men married to sisters) is a matter of congeniality. But, like it or not, close relations between their wives will normally throw *biras* together.

Above all, *biras* stand together as *orang semanda* with regard to a particular *perut*. For ceremonial, although they have no ritual role to play, they must cooperate in the brunt of the work. They also rely on each other for help in tasks such as the building and maintenance of houses. Work on houses is seen as concerned with the welfare of the women and children of the *tempat semanda*. Help given here, therefore, is meeting an obligation to the wife's kin, as well as also helping one's *biras* whose house it is.

Such opportunities for cooperation are, however, limited. Other male economic activities are carried out by individuals, and do not call for the mobilisation of labour, whether by kinship, friendship or hire. Where cooperation is needed, say on rice irrigation works, the work is done by a group wider than any extended family or group of *orang semanda*.

THE NUCLEAR FAMILY AND MATRILINEAL KINSHIP

The villagers of Jelebu hold two principles concerning their social organization which are certainly not consistent, and may give rise to conflict. On the one hand, they stress a man's rights in his own house, his responsibility for, and control over, his wife and children. But, on the other, they subscribe to the contrary matrilineal rule which minimizes the position of the husband/father and emphasizes the role of the mother's brother.

I have already stated what the traditional solution to this social tension is; the husband can either accept the authority of the *tempat semanda* or divorce. Nowadays one cannot predict such an outcome with any confidence. The *tempat semanda* no longer have any strong sanctions against a recalcitrant affine, and a breach with the wife's kin, meaning that one's wife and children are excluded from the *adat* system, is no longer the serious matter it would once have been.

In some cases of conflict the wife has supported her husband. Difficulties arise only when the man wishes to carry out wedding or circumcision ceremonials for his children. If possible a reconciliation will be effected then; if not, the ceremonial will be carried out with the aid of kin not immediately involved, or who supported the family when it broke away. But ceremonies carried out without the full participation of the kin-group require help from kin and friends of the husband who should normally only appear as guests or give peripheral help, and this deviation from tradition is felt to lessen the value of the ceremony.

The influence of *adat* can be clearly seen in the form quarrels between *orang semanda* and *tempat semanda* take. The husband will rarely defend himself openly. There is no answer to the charge, 'this is not part of your father's inheritance'. This is a reminder that the homestead on which he lives, the field from which he gets his rice, are not his own but belong to his wife's kin. I have noticed that when the quarrel takes the form of an exchange of abuse the husband remains silent, leaving his wife to answer her brother or cousins. In one example which concluded a long series of provocations by a wife's brother who had come to live on sub-clan land, his brothers-in-law always endeavoured to avoid conflict with him, ignoring his abuse for example, while his sisters and cousins replied in kind, and even offered him violence. When the *orang semanda* could no longer tolerate his behaviour, they called back their sons on leave from the police, to tell their uncle he must move, and to move his house for him; 'they are of the same *perut*, we cannot interfere in this matter'. A husband quarrelling with his wife's kin is generally forced on the defensive. The mere fact of disagreement with the *tempat semanda* puts him in a weak position. If he does not like the treatment given him he should divorce and leave.

Closer inspection often reveals that what appears a difference between the *tempat semanda* and *orang semanda* is rather a difference within the *orang semanda*. Bad feelings are always likely to arise between a man and his son-in-law. To the son-in-law the conflict will seem to be with the *tempat semanda*, and he will refer to it in this way. Both the husband and father are *orang semanda*, but in such disputes the father is treated as if he were one of the *tempat semanda* or as if he were their representative. (Although it is not commonly used, there is a term *pak manda* to refer to such a senior responsible member of the *orang semanda*.) He has, after all, had a much longer contact with the *tempat semanda*, he is the father of some, and the uncle by marriage of others, and this entitles him to support against a relative newcomer.

There is one kinship term which seems to reflect the special status of an *orang semanda* who is senior, and so parent or grand-parent to many members of the *tempat semanda*, and accordingly entitled to respect and affectionate obedience under family rules if not according to matrilineal *adat*. The mother's father is re-ferred to, and addressed as *dato aki*, the term for all male kin of the parents' parents' generation, with a suffix making it specific to one individual. This is one of two kinship terms particular to Negri Sembilan, the other, *wan*, is used for all grandmothers. For all other relationships terminology follows standard Malay usage.

In attempting to draw a developmental picture the main diffi-culty is to know how the traditional system actually operated. The reminiscences of informants suggest that there has been a shift towards stressing the importance and independence of the nuclear family. This would be an obvious conclusion, given the knowledge we have on the decline of *adat* as a political system. What is difficult is to know how important this shift has been. Thus, one informant has described to me at length his deceased father's continual toleration of exploitation and bad behaviour on the part of his wife's younger brother, because, under the stronger *adat* of those days, there was no way to repulse him without also divorcing my informant's mother. Also the husband, on occasions, gave feasts and paid fines, thereby admitting that he was in the wrong, rather than divorce. On the other hand, when relations with the wife's kin got particularly bad, he built another house on land he had bought and moved there, ignoring the *tempat semanda* until relations improved, when he moved back. These events took place before the 'German War' (pre-1914) when the power of the *lembaga* was still great, and yet we see the hus-band–wife tie able to persist even at the expense of the matri-lineal group. Such information is not sufficient to support any generalizations, and can easily be matched with cases where divorce did result. But it does mean that care must be exercised in assuming that the situation today represents too radical a contrast with the situation a few decades ago.

It is useful, in discussing the relations between the family and the *perut*, to distinguish the levels of structure and organization (Firth, 1951, p. 35). At the level of structure there is an inconsistency in the social system, and one which, since it relates to important and directly connected aspects of the society, must often be productive of tension. At the level of organization we are confronted with the fact that things proceed more or less peacefully. Thus, either the conflicting principles can be harmonized in practice or one must be subordinated to the other. Where the observer is familiar with the personalities and circumstances of a case he will have little difficulty in understanding its development. But at the same time it is impossible to state, *in general*, which principle will be subordinated when there is conflict between them. External pressures (external to the field of face-to-face relations discussed here) are acting to remove this inconsistency from the social structure. Gradually matrilineality will give way to a bilateral form of organization similar to that of other Malays. But the completion of this process lies in the future, and the problems of choice which this structural dilemma occasion are still real to the villager.

CHAPTER XI

The Village, Status and Social Stratification

THE VILLAGE

Just as a number of nuclear families are grouped in extended families, so, in turn, a number of extended families form a village. The unimportance of the village as a social group is seen in the primacy of other group loyalties in the values of the people (as judged by direct statements about loyalties made by informants, and their views on these matters implied in other judgements), and the fact that there is no important activity which relies for its organizational base on recruitment by village.

Jelebu villages have names and boundaries, and a villager can usually tell you where these are; although villages are not clearly nucleated there are, nevertheless, some ecological features which separate them. In some places, where the land rises steeply from the valley floor, there is no land suitable for house sites and a break in the strip of houses running along the valley edge. In other cases, where houses follow a tributary of the main river away from the valley and main road, the valley of a tributary stream will form a boundary between villages on opposite sides. Again, in some cases rubber holdings come right down to the ricefields or road, so that the land is not available for house sites.

The inhabitants of a village use the same path to the roadside, the same coffee and provision shop, the same bus stop. These help to channel their social contacts more towards each other and away from outsiders.

Village sentiments are phrased in much the same way as those attached to the correct relationship between members of a kin-group. Friendliness, cooperation and generosity are admired; envy, unfriendliness and precise calculation in economic matters disapproved. Informants might remark, 'There are no other people here,' i.e. we are all kin. If I asked how this could be so, they replied 'Well, we are all *biduanda*.' This was more nearly true, although not what had been implied in the first place.

The village, as a unit, does not have a clear place in the people's conception of their society. The word *kampong*, although translated as village, is not so precise. A man speaking of his *kampong* may mean the site of his house, his mother's house, the few houses which surround his, or the 'Village', or he may even be referring to a whole locality. In the past the use of the term would not have been so ambiguous. When population was sparser a series of small hamlets, named after some tree or other local feature, each contained the houses of one matrilineal group. In those circumstances the identification of the village with the matrilineal group was appropriate. With population growth these hamlets have merged as houses have been built on the land which used to separate them.

I have mentioned the importance of the peer group for the adolescent youth. For this group the village is a reality. For a few years the boy sees himself as a member of a group (*geng*) recruited from the youth of his village, which is in opposition to the *geng* of other villages.

In the traditional polity the village played no part as such. Nor does it in the modern administration. It is true that this is based on territorial units. But the *ketua kampong* is not a village head. A *mukim* comprising many named villages will have only two or three *ketua kampong*. They are assistants to the *penghulu* with respect to half or a third of the *mukim* rather than village heads.

A number of activities or associations would seem to recruit the members on a village basis, in that most of the members are resident in a particular village. Examples are the funeral benefit association, the group mobilized for cooperative work in rice irrigation, or the men and their families who use one prayer house. But in each case some members will have come from other villages, and some residents of the majority village will not be members.

Traditional ties of kinship are losing their effectiveness. The modernization of Malay society gives rise to a number of activities which require not only technological development but also an organizational framework. The local community provides the rudiments of such a framework, and may be expected to play an increasingly important part in the organization of Malay peasant society. Local elections, rural development schemes, especially under the present drive, cooperative societies, political parties, the parents' associations attached to schools, even the youngsters' '*musik parti*', utilize local groupings. Common residence in a village may not be one of the primary loyalties, but it is a loyalty, and there is a recognition that simply living together in the same village does give common interests and responsibilities.

SOCIAL CLASS

The term social stratification is used here to refer to broad divisions of society differentiated in terms of relative access to the three general categories of value; these are prestige, wealth, and political power. These strata are termed social classes.

The three dimensions of class are those used by Weber in his classic 'Class, Status and Party'. To Weber there were three categories, classes, status groups, and parties, real or potential social groups. I see these categories as elements within a broader concept of class, useful in analysing the nature of any social class. Situations in which a class of people are highly placed in terms of one variable but not another are regarded as being in disequilibrium. Prestige, wealth and power are assumed to be general human values, and it is assumed that the possession of political power will be used to acquire wealth and prestige, or wealth for prestige and power, and so on.

TRADITIONAL MALAY CLASS STRUCTURE

The people of Negri Sembilan share in the tradition of kingship derived from Malaka and Pagar Ruyong. It is therefore desirable to preface the discussion of Negri Sembilan with a brief account of the class system in the Sultanates. Such an account must leave many questions unanswered. The evidence of classical literature (e.g. Sejarah) and historical writings (Gullick, 1958) only allows us to draw a broad picture of a society divided into four classes.

An hereditary royal class headed each Malay State. There was no legitimate possibility of upward mobility into this class, and although some *raja* might fall into great poverty, they still retained the cachet of their birth to warrant a feeling of superiority over the richest and most powerful non-*raja*. Only one category of persons was admitted as the equal of a *raja*, the *syed* descendants of the Prophet. The second class was the non-royal aristocracy, the most important members of which were the District Chiefs or officials of the Sultanate. Together royalty and the aristocracy form a highly privileged upper stratum, the distinction between them made not in terms of the two objective criteria of class, but rather of the subjective factor of prestige, specifically the fact of royal birth.

Among the non-aristocratic elements of the society there are again two classes to be discerned, also distinguished not in terms of wealth or power, but by the subjective evaluation of their position. These were the free peasantry, on the one hand, and the debt bondsmen on the other. (Slavery was also known, but the illegality of enslaving Muslims should mean that slaves were outsiders to Malay society.) For a free peasant to move into bondage was easy, especially in times of unrest, and theoretically all a bondsman had to do to rise was to redeem his loan. Although there was some upward movement into the non-royal aristocracy, and also presumably decline into the peasantry, upward mobility into the aristocracy must be regarded as an exceptional reward for exceptional ability or luck, rather than as a legitimate goal potentially open to anyone.

NEGRI SEMBILAN

In Negri Sembilan prestige was accorded to people of royal descent. This may be seen in the establishment of the royal enclaves at Sri Menanti, Tampin and Jelebu. But the *raja* could not achieve the same power in Negri Sembilan that they could in a Sultanate. Their attempts to do so, and the attempts of the *adat* chiefs to arrogate to themselves the prerogatives of a *raja* (both following from the equilibrium theory) can explain much of the history of the State.

Under *adat perpateh* there was no non-royal aristocracy of hereditary district chiefs and their kin. Emphasis is placed on the kinship group as a unit, and there is no room in the *adat* for institutionalized superiority and inferiority within this group.[1]

---

[1] One of the most striking contrasts I found between *adat* in Jelebu and Minangkabau was the institutionalization of superiority and inferiority within the kin-group in the latter area. There chiefly rank is ideally inherited by the real sister's son, families within the kin-group are said to have high or low inheritance (*pusaka tinggi* and *pusaka rendah*), some members of the group are spoken of as 'sister's sons beneath the knee' (*kemanakan di-bawah lutut*) to fetch whatever is distant and carry whatever is heavy. Similarly there is the distinction between the *orang empat djenis* (the four varieties of people) implicitly of good descent, and *orang ta'berdjenis* people of no variety (of low descent status). Distinctions such as these are quite alien to the ideology of kinship in Jelebu, although, as the discussion of status shows, feelings of superiority and inferiority are not totally absent from the social organization.

Nevertheless, I believe that in fact there was such a system of inequality. I have already discussed the importance of wealth and the connections of kinship and affinity in deciding succession to *adat* office. These factors readily create a situation where a few families, by influence and arranged marriages, can monopolize succession to kinship office over the generations. Study of the kinship connections of present chiefs, and even shallow genealogies, soon make this apparent. This tendency to class formation is important in understanding the operation of the society, but it is wrong to conclude that it comes to 'much the same thing' as the class divisions of the Sultanate. Status divisions in Negri Sembilan were neither as rigid nor as great as those in the other Malay States, and above all, they were in conflict with the basic ideology of the society which saw all relations within the *waris* and *perut* as based on the model of relations within a family.

In the same way, the foundation of society on kinship precluded the extensive development of the relationships of debt bondage and slavery. Redeeming a kinsman who had fallen into debt was, indeed, one of the few reasons for which *pusaka* property might be sold.

In summary then, traditional Negri Sembilan society accorded prestige to royal descent, but neither political power, nor the wealth which might be derived from such power, to the *raja* living amongst them. Within the broad mass of the population a superior class position was enjoyed by those possessing wealth and *adat* office. This is to be regarded as evidence of class, rather than merely individual status differences, because of the tendency for these differences to be transmitted, on a family basis, from generation to generation.

MODERN DEVELOPMENTS

Wertheim's work (1956, pp. 133ff.) distinguishes two forces which tended to disrupt the status system of nineteenth-century Indonesia. First there was the growth of modern administration, and technological developments demanding an educated personnel for their operation. This led to the emergence of what amounts to a certificate-holding elite. Secondly the commercialization of the economy gave rise to a new class of wealthy villagers who challenged the authority and prestige of the traditional chiefs.

How far can these findings be applied to the situation in Malay society?

That referring to the growth of an elite of western education may be transferred almost directly to Malaya. The superiority of the modern administrative system has meant the superiority of the official. The upper-class figures of Malay society today are largely Government officials and their families, who have achieved their positions, in part at least, through their possession of a western education.

One difference between Malay and Indonesia arises in connection with Indian immigration into Malaya. The Indian has filled two roles of great importance. First, the Indian is the wage labourer in government employment and on rubber estates. In Indonesia these tasks were undertaken by Indonesians and in Malaya would presumably have fallen to Malays but for the availability of Indians. Also Indians were recruited, already trained, for technical and clerical posts, so that a Department such as the Public Works Department seems entirely Indian in both labouring and supervisory grades. These technical and clerical posts would also presumably have been filled by Malays. The educated Chinese was not, until recently, attracted by Government service, and Chinese labourers would not work for the low pay of an Indian labourer. They preferred to work harder, for more money, in contracting work or tin mining, rather than the regular, slow, but poorly paid, work of the road mender. The differentiation of the economy by ethnic group in a plural society has insulated Malay society from the full impact of the changes which have been affecting Malaya.

There is some continuity between the old aristocracy and the modern upper class. The close kin of a sultan or major chief are well placed to acquire education, and likely to be favourably regarded when they come to seek employment. The most important institution for the preparation of Malays for senior posts in the Government service (at least prior to the opening of the University of Malaya) was the Malay College at Kuala Kangsar, originally intended to provide education for the sons of aristocrats so that they might enter the administration.

The above remarks apply to Malay society as a whole. Where I feel Negri Sembilan differs from the general pattern is in the relative failure of the local chiefs and wealthy men to secure for their children the education which could win them entry into the upper class. This may reflect the relative lack of differentiation of traditional society. Certainly this 'backwardness' is the case in Jelebu; it is partly to be explained by the attitude of the former *Undang* Dato Abdullah whose reign covered a crucial period in this development. However, this means that the upper class of Jelebu is of relatively low status according to the ranking of the wider society, rather than different in kind.

The same importance cannot be accorded Wertheim's second factor where Negri Sembilan is concerned. The commercialization of the economy, especially the cultivation of rubber, offers greater opportunities for the accumulation of wealth than a subsistence economy. But as the chiefs of Negri Sembilan did not form a hereditary group economic differentiation did not give rise to an overt clash with the new rich demanding equality with the chiefs. In a kin-group the man who has accumulated wealth has the opportunity to add a title to give his wealth the finish of prestige. Conversely, however well connected a man might be he would be unlikely to succeed to an office if he were too poor, nor, knowing that he laid himself open to shame, would he be likely to wish to do so.

Traditionally the institution of *menyeraya*, gifts from his kin for feasts, and his control of the clan lands, would help a chief, once installed, maintain his position of economic superiority. The loss of these rights, and the changing nature of the economy, which has made rice a much less important crop, undermined the economic position of the chief, and so weakened his position generally. But these changes, although economic in their consequences, follow from political changes. Economic change in Negri Sembilan has not produced the same type of challenge to the traditional system as that reported from Indonesia (Schrieke, 1956, pp. 95 ff.) and this is to be explained not by any difference in the economic forces involved but by the greater fluidity of the traditional status system.

SOCIAL CLASS IN CONTEMPORARY VILLAGE LIFE

The broadest class divisions recognized by the villagers divide Malay society into two. The larger and lower class is the peasantry (*orang kampong*). Against this class is set an upper class for which there are many designations. They may be called the wealthy (*orang kaya*) or the wage earners (*orang makan gaji*), great or big people (*orang besar*), or perhaps educated people (*orang kerani*) or townsmen (*orang pekan*). None of these terms has the descriptive clarity of the word for villager. They refer to people who work for a living in some official capacity, who therefore possess a modern education, generally live in a town, and follow a westernized style of life.

Compared with this class the peasantry see themselves as poor and uninfluential, living a hard and useful life (for they grow food, the basis of everything), more worthy and moral than the town dweller. The town dweller or official has no understanding of the problems of the peasantry, they say, and he does not care about them for he is only concerned with his own wealth and status. Such hostile attitudes, often expressed, do not preclude the greatest deference when a peasant confronts a member of the upper class.

To some extent the upper class accept the peasants' estimation of their own worth. It is true that the peasant is despised as ignorant and superstitious, but the Malay Government official also recognizes that in some way the peasant has a more worthwhile life, and possesses important, and perhaps specifically Malay, virtues. Moreover, although the official lives in a town he may well have been born in a village where he maintains his connection with relatives and may intend to retire. This will not be true to the same extent of the next generation of officials, brought up in their parents' urban quarters, but for the time being it is still reasonable to characterize the Malay as an essentially rural people, especially in contrast with the other races which have settled in Malaya. Even Malay urban settlements, such as Kampong Bahru in Kuala Lumpur, and the Malay Settlement in Singapore, retain their village air. The Malay official strikes one as eager to air his knowledge of rice, or his appreciation of the various wild leaves which may be eaten as vegetables. The villager is felt to be the real Malay. At a time of intense nationalism, the man who is too advanced and urban is denying his race, his religion and culture, and identifying with the alien people of the town.

The official's romantic stereotype of village life stresses the spirit of friendliness and cooperation which is supposed to underlie life there, and compares it with the anonymity and self-seeking of the town. In fact, although in some situations the peasants see themselves as forming a group in a common situation of low status, there are marked differences in class even within the village itself.

The most general and acceptable basis of claims to superior status in the village is wealth. According to their standing by this criterion villagers are allocated positions on a three-class scale. At the top are found a few villagers recognized as prominent or rich. The majority are ordinary, and at the bottom are a few not worth consideration (*bangsat*). From the point of view of prestige, deference and contempt are accorded to individuals not by placing them in direct relation to others, but by rating them as rich, ordinary, and poor. There are recognizable status symbols constituting a style of life. Economic gradings then are evaluated in moral (prestige) terms. As far as the power dimension is concerned, everyone in the village may be said to be under-privileged in that respect with regard to the wider society, but within the small field of community decisions, power is also closely related to an individual's economic standing.

The precise expression given to these prestige ideas naturally varies with the individual informant's own place in the scale. The rich feel that they have merely achieved the just reward for their superior abilities and character, while their less successful neighbours place more emphasis on luck, and on meanness and hardness in personal relations. The poor blame their own lot on bad luck, or on some bad turn played them by others, while to other villagers their position is liable to be seen as the result of laziness, thriftlessness or some other personal weakness.

There is much substance in the view which regards the individual's lot as his own making. In this society, where standards of living are generally low, the difference between grades in terms of income is not large. To be wealthier than average does require more than average industry and care in disposing of one's income. Even if one derives a sizeable inheritance from one's father, not everyone can resist the temptation to sell it in order to raise consumption. There are no really large inherited fortunes such as would make competition for status meaningless for most people; although inheriting rubber land is a great advantage under present conditions when holdings can only be acquired through purchase or inheritance, since Government land alienation policy precludes a poor but industrious peasant directly acquiring property through developing his own rubber holding. In the same way, if a man is not incapacitated, to be poorer than average he must be lazy. Where most incomes are derived from rubber tapping anyone who is fit can tap, and can receive an income sufficient to lead a respectable life as an ordinary villager, not respected for his wealth, it is true, but not despised for his poverty either.

These class ideas can thus be seen to have important functional consequences; where there is some measure of equality of opportunity the prestige evaluation of wealth gives a direct incentive to production. This effect is not absolute however. The importance of the rich man is recognized but he is far from popular. Too obvious economic success opens the way for bad relations with kin and neighbours. The newly rising man runs a great risk of shame if he blossoms too quickly with the symbols of his new status. Everyone will be watching for his first mistake, and longing for the day when he defaults on his hire-purchase payments and the Chinese comes to take his goods away.

Community life in a small village requires that too great differences in wealth be avoided. The ties of reciprocity based on small loans and gifts of goods, and on small exchanges of services, are endangered when some of the participants are much poorer, or much richer, than average. The poor obviously cannot reciprocate the gifts they receive. One way in which this difficulty is avoided is for a poor family to accept quasi-dependent status with a wealthier family. The wealthy family allow the poor to borrow when in need, although there is no hope of repayment, and the poorer family provides help when the richer gives a feast, or when the householder has a job of work to do, such as repairing the house, which needs more than his own labour. The dependent family will also support the richer family if there is conflict within the village. Such dependants may be kin or they may not (close kin; in one way or another everyone in this society is kin). But the relationship creates resentment too. The poor wish to be regarded as neighbours who are helping out, and do not like the occasionally arrogant attitude the richer family adopts towards them, when, for example, children of the richer family tease adults of the poorer and call them by name rather than by a kin term. The richer family, on the other hand, feels the continual demands of the poor as parasitism, a charity which is not properly appreciated by the recipients. The relationship is not institution-alized clientship but implicit in the social structure. It is important in allowing a special position to the wealthier families which they could not afford if they had to pay money for the services they receive. Also, of course, it makes it possible for poor families to manage through periods of difficulty.

The relations of the rich with villagers not poor enough to be dependants are also not good. The strength of bitterness and jealousy is striking. These emotions have to be taken as a psycho-logical given here, but it is, I feel, possible to point to a socio-logical element in them which helps to account for the nature of the emotions if not their strength. The rich are the obvious source of material help, but since there are only a few of them in each village they are continually subject to demands, while they do not have occasion to seek help themselves. The recipients accept the help they give not with gratitude, but as a right, for the rich are their kin, or their neighbours, and they are wealthy; a small gift is nothing to them. This one-sided relationship creates re-sentment, for the rich resent having to give all the time while their good nature is not sufficiently recognized. The recipient of help resents having to ask for it, and not receiving more. Two other features of the rich-poor relationship are also relevant. The first refers to the source of the rich man's property. A poor peasant in need of money has little alternative but to sell some land. This land will often be bought by one of the recognized rich men. When the crisis is over, and the need for money less urgently felt, the seller often regrets his bargain, and feels that the buyer took unfair advantage of his difficulties. The second concerns the chara-ter of richer men. Some men owe their superior position to re-taining a good proportion of a larger than average inheritance, thus getting the all important surplus which permits further land purchase, and a larger surplus. But others have become rich with-out a special start. Such people must show special drive, and also a disregard for the opinions of others, for these demand gener-osity and a concern with non-economic obligations which will prevent accumulation and keep a man down at the common level. Even the man wealthy by inheritance must show these qualities if his wealth is not to be dispersed.

The peasant knows that if he is poor he is regarded with con-tempt and must be ashamed. But he also knows that to strive for success will arouse envy and resentment. For the ordinary man, sensitive to the feelings of his kin and neighbours, there are strong motives to keep him up to the normal income level, but also important pressures to prevent his making great efforts to rise beyond this point.

These values apply primarily to fellow villagers. Jealousy and envy are not directed to the same extent against the upper class of officials. A grander style of life is held to be their right. Thus egalitarian values are not radical, demanding a change in the whole organization of society, but rather conservative, concerned with maintaining existing distinctions and limiting individual mobility. There is, of course, considerable expression of hostility against the official class, but the attitude is ambivalent, hostility being combined with respect and an admission of their superiority.

Their possessions mark the style of life of the village upper class. The rich peasant has a large well-made house that nowadays costs upwards of $5,000. Within the house the furnishings of the verandah, where male guests are received, are the surest indicator of class. These should include a set of chairs and a glass topped table, a glass-fronted cupboard or two filled with paper flowers, framed photographs, and such other ornaments as may take a Malay's fancy. A radio too is essential, although it is nowadays becoming too common to be a sure indicator of class by itself. In 1954, when I first entered the village, there were only two radios, one of which formed part of the attractions of the coffee-shop, on my last count in 1957 there were eleven.[1]

There is not such a marked distinction between the households of the wealthy and the average villager where consumption in food and clothing are concerned. This is not to say there are no distinctions, but merely that these distinctions do not serve as symbols to set the wealthy man apart from the ordinary villager.

Apart from the prestige accorded to a style of life that is at least partly correlated with wealth, there remains the expression of these class distinctions in community leadership and decision making, the power dimension of class at the village level. The correlation is close. At the time when the major part of this research was carried out representative political institutions had not yet been introduced, and although universal suffrage now

---

[1] The impact of the transistor revolution in integrating the peasant more firmly into a national culture is a worthy topic for research.

makes the Malay peasant the major political force in Malaya he has not yet learned to use his strength. But in matters where the villagers are independent of external control, power clearly lies in the hands of the wealthy upper-class peasants.

As stated before, *adat* office tends to go to the wealthy. The houses of the clan chiefs and of many of the *ibubapa*, demonstrate the style of life of the wealthy peasant. *Ketua kampong* are also mainly of this class, and in some cases where they were not they clearly lacked the authority to carry out their duties effectively. But not all authority and leadership in the village is exercised by office bearers, if only because every village does not necessarily have a representative of either system of authority living within it. Even so, those who emerge as leaders are of the same class standing as the official leaders of *adat* and administration.

The fields where leadership may be exercised may be termed regular or irregular. The prime, almost the sole, example of the first type is the irrigation of the ricefields. When should the dam be built? When should it be closed and the fields flooded? When should it be opened and the fields allowed to dry? In form these are collective decisions, but the actual process of decision-making involves sounding the opinions of the village notables, compromising if there be disagreement, and then informing the other villagers when the date will be. Other villagers can express opinions to the decision-makers and have their views considered, for the aim is to choose dates convenient for everyone lest there be absenteeism and bad feeling, but these other men do not make decisions.

An informal decision by the important villagers, which is then presented to the majority for their approval, might well be called the paradigm of village decision-making. Where rice cultivation is concerned there is little room for division of opinion about timing. No villager is likely to have pressing reasons for disagreeing with the dates proposed, but those who do will be accommodated. With the irregular type of decision however, there is every possibility of wide divergence of opinion.

The following examples of irregular decisions excited village opinion during my stay. The prayer house is in disrepair, should it be repaired or rebuilt? Is it worth while improving the track into the village so that cars can come right in? Should we form a funeral benefit association? Can, or should, the village arrange a special celebration of the Prophet's Birthday? Should we try to get the Department of Drainage and Irrigation to take over the irrigation of our fields, or should we continue with the village dam? Should we, and can we, replace the prayer house with a proper mosque?

With questions such as these action may founder on either an inability to get agreement among the village leaders, or a lack of support from the majority. If disagreement amongst the leaders comes into the open the other villagers take sides on the basis of kinship ties and friendship. Perhaps there will be enough support for the proposers and their supporters to go ahead while a minority conspicuously abstains. For identifiable factions to crystallize they must be led by someone with upper-class qualities. If, however, the leaders are able to agree on some proposal which does not arouse the enthusiasm of the other villagers they will not encounter overt opposition. Simply, when the time comes for collective work many of the villagers will be unable to attend, or when the times comes for collecting subscriptions many of them will be without money. Sensing the opposition behind apparent agreement is an important skill for anyone wishing to exercise leadership in a village.

The question of disagreement over a proposed action raises the issue of the nature of relations within the peasant upper class. They are aware of each other as belonging on the same level above the other villagers. In talking about village affairs a wealthy villager may list the other villagers who matter, and his list will correspond closely with the observer's conclusions based on a study of style of life, or on observations of village decision-making. Also, in arranging marriages the wealthy try to secure a *menantu* from a family of the same standing as their own.

Yet the upper class are also aware of each other as competitors for prestige and position. To some extent each owes his success to a strong drive to surpass the rest. In the accumulation of wealth this competition can be carried on without leading directly to enmity. But when wealth is used for the purchase of status symbols the competition becomes much more personalized, and when competition moves into the field of power (which I see as a 'zero-sum concept'—Parsons, 1960, p. 219) it may be said that one man's success can only be achieved at the direct expense of his competitors. Many village leaders are such because they have striven hard to achieve the position, and in the course of their striving have made bitter enemies. Kinship is important in the formation of these enmities, but the alignments do not directly follow kinship allegiances. It is just as likely that enmity will arise through competition for the control of the kin-group, and spread from there to have village significance.

I shall now discuss relations between the peasantry and those members of the upper official class with whom they come into most frequent contact, that is to say, members of the lower ranks of the Government service. These people may have received little more formal education than many villagers, and have rarely received much English schooling. Malay schoolteachers, some clerks, *penghulu* and their assistants, Assistants in the Department of Agriculture, etc., may be recruited from the more fortunate students of Malay (vernacular) schools. Yet despite their not possessing a markedly superior education there is a clear tendency to accord prestige to these people on the part of the villagers. For even without a certificate, Government service implies a familiarity with modern ways, and an ability to move easily in the atmosphere of town and office, qualities which even the wealthiest of peasants rarely possess. Villagers who are forceful leaders in their own surroundings, become deferential, even abject, when they confront the official world. Officials, on the other hand, may often be picked out by their behaviour at a village gathering. For example, at a wedding in an important village family, where some of the guests are officials, it may be remarked how they gather together and behave themselves in a loud and flamboyant way, in marked contrast with the usual standards of Malay decorum on such occasions.

What is the role of these minor officials in village leadership? Many officials who come from the villages live in town, and some of them may not even be working in the District, and so can only occasionally intervene in village affairs. But teachers, *penghulu*, and some other minor officials live in the village. Although their work and interests give them friendships with others of their kind, they are also involved in the lives of their kin and neighbours. These minor officials are also clearly part of the peasant upper class. (I see them as an interstitial category between peasantry and upper class, belonging, in a sense, to both.) In style of life they follow the same standards as the wealthy peasants, perhaps setting the pace in the striving after modernity. They are often the children of these upper-class peasants, and use their salaries to build up a position of wealth in the village through the accumulation of land. Yet within the village the teachers and the clerk have a higher status than the wealthiest peasant, because, unimportant as they may be when compared with the District Officer, they are, nevertheless, of the official class.

But detachment from the village, which gives them much of their prestige, also disqualifies them from taking leadership to any great extent in the everyday affairs of the village. For one thing they may lack the necessary knowledge of cultivation and building techniques. A schoolteacher when he expresses views probably advocates some new technique he has read about, and is dismissed as impractical, a wage earner who does not know what he is talking about. This is often true. When a schoolmaster is one of a gathering the peasantry are liable to find themselves listening to a monologue about what needs to be done, and why the Malay fails to advance. This is to all intents and purposes a condemnation of the capabilities and industry of the villagers, his listeners. Malays respect teachers; even the lowliest is addressed as Mr. Teacher, and so the teacher's audience will not contradict him, but, should he be the first to leave, they will round on him in his absence. 'That's fine talk, but just talk.' 'If he knew the heat of the ricefields he would not have so much to say.' 'If I had big wages then I would know how to tell people what to do.' Again, the people love to discuss religion. Here the teacher often finds himself in opposition to the views of most peasants, advocating reforms and attacking practices which are dear to the hearts of the peasants, which *are* religion to them.

A teacher or clerk can exercise influence in village affairs to the extent that he is prepared to be like the peasants in his interests and values. But since his interests and values were moulded in the same process which gave him his post and the qualities giving him extra prestige in the village, few teachers can make the necessary adjustments.

An occasional exception to this rule can be found in the irregular type of coactivity. In 1954 two villages combined for a celebration of the Prophet's Birthday. This involved a large tea party in the afternoon, at which an address was given by a prominent religious teacher from outside the District, and a recital of Koranic reading and Arabic songs by her pupils. In the evening the more traditional *Maulud Nabi* took place. The initiative came from a small group of schoolteachers and clerks, who chose the visiting performers and made arrangements for them to come. When problems such as building a stage and the preparation of food arose, bad feeling split this group from the mass of the villagers. The peasants thought the initiators did not understand matters such as the organization of collective work and had too grandiose notions about the scale of preparations, refreshments and cash contributions which might reasonably be expected. A further source of disagreement flowing from the difference in attitude of the modern and the peasant groups was the proposal to include *Maulud Nabi* in the celebration. To the peasants this seemed very fitting, but it was strongly opposed on doctrinal grounds by some of the teachers.

Another example, which did not give rise so clearly to peasant-official conflict, although the strain was there, comes from the field of economic cooperation. Over the past seven years (1960) a cooperative rice-milling society has been in operation. During this time a mobile rice mill and a tractor bought on loan have been paid off, additional equipment, land (including a town site) and buildings purchased, and a cash balance built up too. This is an outstanding achievement in a field where failure is all too common.

The original proposal came from the Government, working through villagers who were recognized as progressive and influential. The operations of the society have at all times been guided by the RIDA Cooperative Officer, although the failure of similar societies elsewhere shows that this, in itself, is no guarantee of success. In fact, the society is a genuine cooperative, decisions are made by an elected committee and on no important point have they been overruled by the cooperative officer. All the officials are villagers, but they are not ordinary villagers, in that most of them have had an unusual degree of contract with the administration, in posts such as *penghulu*, assistant *penghulu*, schoolteacher or *ketua kampong*. These people have kept the society sound. They have adopted a policy of reinvestment and resisted demands for the division of the profits. They have also resisted most attempts at nepotism in the appointment of employees, and have not adopted the usual casual village standards with regard to carelessness over accounts and dishonesty. Also their experience of committee procedure has been an asset.

Their success is the result of experience and values acquired in Government service; without this they would have fallen into the same snares as have led to the failure of so many other cooperative societies. And it was their prestige, derived from the same Government service, which led to their election to the committee.

These examples are meant to show the importance of the prestige attached to the official with his modern training and outlook. It is from such people that new ideas reach the villagers, and, because of the superior position of the innovators, have a better chance of success. Another important aspect of this innovatory role is in the field of party politics. The elections of 1957 and 1959 clearly showed that the United Malay Nationalist Organization (UMNO) had the massive support of the villagers, and this is as true of Jelebu as elsewhere. The party was formed out of a number of existing Malay organizations in 1946 in response to the threat to the Malays of the Malayan Union. Villagers said that the party was greeted with great enthusiasm and 'all' men became members. Branch committee members often came from the peasant upper class, but the officers were nearly all representatives of the official class, to such an extent that it seemed almost a tradition for the senior Malay Government Officer in the District to be the chairman.

In 1954 Government forbade officers of grades 1, 2 and 3 to engage in political activity or hold party office. This robbed the movement of many important officers, but party office still remained with the official class, now with petty officials instead of with the higher ranks. Even before this the party had lost much of its enthusiastic mass support. Members did not resign; as the elections have shown few of them transferred their political loyalties elsewhere. They simply ceased to attend meetings and to pay their subscriptions. Many branches collapsed entirely, while others just managed to survive through the efforts of a few activists, amongst whom schoolteachers were an important element.

This is of importance because the UMNO is the major partner in the governing Alliance party. The voice of the branches, which must play some part in determining policy, is therefore largely the voice of a particular section of the Malays, those activists, largely of modern education and employment but of minor rank, who run the various branches. Many of these people are in close touch with the peasantry, coming from them and living amongst them; yet they are no longer peasants, and differ from them in attitudes and interests in important respects. This is one reason why dissatisfaction with UMNO has become vocal in the villages.

The high prestige attached to Government employment is enjoyed only by the holders of clerical and other white collar jobs. Many villagers are, or have been, policemen and soldiers. Others are lorry drivers, postmen, or labourers for the Public Works, Drainage and Irrigation, or Agricultural Departments. These posts do not confer any particular prestige; they are re-garded as just like village work. If anything, labouring work is thought to be best left to Tamils.

Education helps to determine class position in the village as well as in the wider society. Yet a wealthy peasant rarely attempts to secure it for his child. This is not solely a question of expense. Malay parents will readily spend to indulge a child. Rather, this failure to avail themselves of opportunities for upward mobility for their children is an indication of the extent to which a class outlook on society determines perception and goals. A man is a peasant, so his children are peasants. This makes peasant remarks about the nature of society into self-fulfilling prophecies. Thus, at the time of the elections there was a vogue for cynical remarks saying that elections made no difference, the people on top would still be on top, and those at the bottom still at the bottom.

Even when a child is enrolled in an English school there is no pressure on him at home to succeed. He may even be told not to over-tax his brain! A poor report is received with sympathy rather than anger, a marked contrast to the severity of discipline in Koranic studies, even when the father is teacher. When failure eventually causes the child to leave school his parents' reaction seems to be more relief than regret, 'after all, we are village people and it is better we stay in the village'. This in a society where great opportunity awaits the Malay who can achieve the necessary scholastic standards, given the shortage of trained personnel in a rapidly changing society, and the preferential treatment given to Malays in filling posts.

On the other hand, jobs which are seen as appropriate for village youth, such as police service, the armed forces, junior posts in the technical departments or as office boys, are eagerly sought; parents can be reconciled to their sons seeking them, and often want a wage earner as a son-in-law. It is the same feeling which accepts as fitting political leadership from outside the peasantry, while at the same time complaining that the party has betrayed them.

INDIVIDUAL STATUS

In village society most social relations are personalized. The same individuals are met in a variety of activities and performing a variety of roles. Great emphasis is therefore placed on personal qualities, and reactions to a given individual, while partially determined by the institutional definition of role behaviour, are also very much affected by likes and dislikes, respect and contempt, flowing from personal qualities which cut across class position, and influence the rating of an individual within his class.

Age entitles one to respect, but outside the family context this factor is weaker than class position in determining the treatment accorded to an individual.

A good man should be a hard worker, but he must also have time to stop and say a few words to friends and neighbours, and to meet the demands of feasts and ceremonies. He must manage his personal relations with dignity. A man who quarrels with his wife in such a way that other people know about it, who scolds and abuses his children, and engages in noisy quarrels with people who offend him, is a fool and contemptible. Getting excited, and speaking wildly, even when one does not offend anyone, places one's judgement in doubt, and gives rise to the suspicion that one is *tiga suku* (three-quarters – 'a bit missing').

Generosity is important, but perhaps more for avoiding the resentment which follows not being generous, rather than for any positive increase in status as a recognition of generosity. Generosity brings supernatural reward (*pahala*), and the villagers, discussing an act of charity, often seem to regard it more as a purchase of *pahala* than a laudable act in this world.

In drawing this picture of the respectable village man I have made no mention of piety or religious knowledge. The relevance of religious qualification for status in the village is of some interest in Malay sociology. The popular idea, even amongst educated Malays, is that the villagers have such great respect for religious teachers (*ulama*) that they can be regarded as a sort of aristocracy and high-influence group amongst the peasants.

For Jelebu at least this is not so. In most villages there are individuals noted for their religious knowledge and ability to read the appropriate prayers at feasts. They are invited to more feasts than other people, are seated in a place of honour when they attend, and may be selected for *fitrah* payments. In the context of religion, then, they receive status recognition. But it is not correct to conclude from this that they have a generally high status in all situations. A man who is in demand at his neighbours' feasts for his prayers, and who is a *haji*, may still be regarded as an old rogue, and it is this last judgement which determines his individual status.

Indeed, the general stereotype of the pious and the religious teachers is rather hostile. The teacher is regarded as someone who sells religion, since he derives his living from it, and as especially untrustworthy with women pupils. Whatever he tells you to do is concerned with better opportunities for him to get 'charity'. Such judgements are not usually made of local men of religious eminence, for few of them are professionals, but they were frequently heard when visiting notables or past visitors to the District were under discussion. A pious man too is liable to be criticized as a hypocrite. A favourite comment is that prayers and fasting are of no use if the heart is not true. This is an aspect of the people's opposition to formalism in religion. The features of Islam which can be observed throughout Malaya are also to be found in Jelebu, but to a less marked extent. For example, the Pilgrimage; in Jelebu a few people have been to Mecca, and a few others will express a desire to go, but most peasants, even those whom I judge could well afford the journey, say that they are not ready. I found this a marked contrast with Malays elsewhere.

For the highest religious dignitary in the District, the *Kadi*, there is great respect. This also applies to the growing group of Religious Affairs Department officials. These people, however, obviously qualify for upper-class status in any case. The respect which is accorded an upper-class man who has been to Mecca, and who is scrupulous in religious observance, may seem to be respect for his religious qualities. But should his position be compared with that of a poor man of similar religious qualification it becomes apparent that this respect, while perhaps differing in form, does not differ in foundation from that given other members of the upper class, for there is no special recognition for the poor and the pious.

Elsewhere in Malaya I have been impressed by the role played by religion in the organization of the community. The meeting at the mosque or prayer house (*surau*, or *manda'sah* in the north) is the principle means of organizing village cooperation, whether for religion or other purposes (S. Hussin Ali, 1960). The village there is more purely a territorial unit for it does not have the complex interrelationship with kinship grouping of the Jelebu village. Local organization centres upon the mosque or prayer house. In such circumstances the village leaders will tend to be prominent in mosque affairs, and the religiously qualified, through their position in the mosque, will exercise a wide influence over village affairs generally. In Negri Sembilan it was kinship rather than local groupings which were important. Kinship office was more important for status than religious qualification, and the meeting of the kin-group rather than of a local group organized coactivity. *Adat* could also provide a substitute for religion in another context, that of providing intellectual satisfaction and interest. *Adat* involved first of all a system of rules which could be debated in themselves and in their particular application, but it also contains a rich body of myths and magical ideas, and I found that it was these which interested many *adat* experts rather than formal rules of social organization.

Two other village specialists are also treated with deference in particular situations. These are the *pawang* and the *dukun*, both of whom I shall call magicians. Rice cultivation, housebuilding, personal or collective misfortune and sickness require the services of a magician. Many men know a few spells which they will use for the benefit of their kin and neighbours, but to be acknowledged a magician must have extensive knowledge and wide reputation. Magic can be a very profitable occupation to the successful magician, and he may be called to carry out cures throughout the State and even further, for people seem more inclined to trust a magician from another place. But for all that his high status is confined to the context of his profession. People follow his orders about treatment (and prohibitions are a very important part of Malay healing), and treat him with deference during the actual magical performance, but in other contexts it is his class position and character which determine his status, the influence he can exert on the community, and the deference shown him. People are ambivalent in their attitude to magicians, and often express this in stories of magicians who came to a bad end through not being able to control the supernatural forces with whom they trafficked, or through falling into the temptation to put their knowledge to evil ends. It is also common knowledge that the magician's earnings, however large, cannot bring him peace and happiness (*duit panas, ta'kan selamat*).

There is another specialist whose status is an interesting indicator of the character of the society. In the town, conveniently near the Government Offices and the Law Court, the petition writer plies his trade. Land transfers, applications for land or licences, contracts, all require a higher standard of literacy than many peasants possess, especially when much of the correspondence is carried on in English. Also, a knowledge of administrative procedure is important if such transactions are to be successfully concluded. These the petition writer supplies.

He may be someone who has retired from Government service, or someone who was unable to complete his education and secure employment, or even someone who had been employed and lost his post through some misdemeanour. His success depends a great deal on maintaining close contacts with Government clerks, if only to secure a supply of blank forms, but despite his cultural similarity with the elite he is not highly regarded by them. In the town the petition writer is marginal to the social circle of the clerks and other officers. But in the village he is treated as a member of the modern group, and accepted as such by its representatives living there.

This discussion of status and social stratification has added the final dimension to our model of village social structure. Each villager occupies a position in a system of kinship ties, of local and domestic groupings, and finally within the class system, and his social life is a resultant of all three.

Kinship organization is in decline, and marked changes have taken place even within the memory of a middle aged man. Local organization, on the other hand, has become more important. Yet this is not the simple substitution of local for kinship organization. The process of decline in the kinship structure has coincided with the removal from peasant control of many institutions which have become the province of the administration.

In social stratification the major change has been the growth of a modern educated official class along with the extension of administration. To a certain extent this may be depicted as an additional layer placed on top of village society. Within the village stratification is still largely based on economic position, tempered by the basically equalitarian kinship organization.

CHAPTER XII

Economy and Society

The small scale of organization is the most striking social feature of the peasant economy. In all important economic activities either the individual or the husband–wife team is the producing unit. Activities mobilizing a larger group are nowadays usually the response to an emergency, as when labour must be hired for the rice harvest, or planting done through the use of *menyeraya*.

Both the highly developed ethnic specialization of the Malayan economy, and the type of good produced in the village economy, favour this lack of large-scale organization. If economic functions such as transport, merchandising, finance, and the processing of primary products were not carried on by the Chinese, Europeans and Indians, Malay society would either have to develop more complex organizational forms to handle these functions, or have a different economy.

In addition there are features of the society itself which militate against large-scale organization. The first of these is the weakness of traditional groupings. The clan and subclan did not engage in any major forms of co-activity which would give them qualities suitable for adaptation to modern economic tasks. It is true that in the nineteenth century some of the chiefs engaged in small-scale tin mining, but in general the kin groups were primarily regulatory in function. Ceremonies and feasts were the only major activities involving efficient organization in which they were engaged, and such activity is intermittent. This intermittent character of kinship organization is increased by matrilocality. The most important members of most kin-groups are the adult males, and unlike the situation in a patrilineal corporate group where the adult males are continuously together, under *adat perpateh* the kinship group is mobilized only occasionally.

Modern political changes have aggravated the weakness of traditional groupings, taking away the regulatory functions of the kin-groups and weakening the authority of the chiefs. The lack of any clear system of legitimate authority in the contemporary village is one of the major factors inhibiting organization. Even acephalous cooperation for simple, generally acceptable tasks within the village is obstructed by competition for leadership positions amongst a variety of pretenders, basing their claims on the several criteria of prestige valid in the village. Granted that most claimants will fall within the richer group of upper-class peasants there remains ample room for competition between them.

One of the most direct connections between the economy and other areas of the social structure is seen in status and social stratification. The major class distinction between peasant and official has an important economic dimension in that official salaries are normally higher than peasant incomes, and a high income is necessary for a modern 'style of life'. But the importance attached to governmental position and education in themselves prevent us regarding this class distinction as a purely economic one. Within the peasant class however the distinctions made are almost entirely economic; even the terms used for prestige gradings are rich, ordinary, and poor.

Studying the economy as an autonomous sector of the social structure we can show that there is an internal process making for the concentration of ownership in a few hands, with a corresponding increase in the economic differentiation of the society. Given the importance attached to wealth in the status system it follows that there will be a move away from equalitarianism in the peasant society, and assuming this trend to continue unaffected by other forces, what will be seen is an increasingly large class of low status share-tappers, and a small group of wealthy men controlling an increasingly large share of the society's productive assets.

The scattered evidence throughout Malaya indicates that this concentration of ownership is a general phenomenon. With regard to Jelebu I have emphasized the effect of Government making land a scarce good by its land alienation policy. Adopting a more general viewpoint I would stress the great and continuing increase in population which has caused a genuine land shortage for much of the country. The formerly low level of population and current population growth provide an explanation of why such a common feature of peasant economies as landlordism and impoverished tenantry are only now beginning to appear in widespread form in Malaya. A further necessary feature of this process is the commercialization of the economy so that all needs and obligations tend to be mediated through money, which from being something which the peasant occasionally uses, in a marginal sector of his economic life apart from his main subsistence activities, becomes necessary for even simple day-to-day survival. In such circumstances the possession of a surplus income over ordinary consumption expenditure assumes enormous significance. The ordinary peasant who does not possess this surplus can only meet extra demands on his resources by selling land. The possessor of a surplus, on the other hand, can not only survive extraordinary expenditures without having to part with his main productive capital, but can also buy the property of others, often at very low prices, when the opportunity arises. As land is now a scarce good, only to be acquired by purchase, and as he has now an even lower income than formerly, the peasant who is forced to sell his land has little real hope of acquiring more, and is confronted with the alternatives of share-cropping or drifting to the town. In this analysis the prime causes of land concentration are therefore (i) land shortage, arising from population growth, which might be temporarily obviated by a more generous land alienation policy, (ii) a largely monetary economic system.

For Jelebu I believe that the concentration process is only beginning, and in this connection I would repeat the point made earlier, of the vital part played by unallocated fruit income as a means of financing expenditures above ordinary daily consumption.

It might be argued that this concentration of ownership is to be explained by technological or other economies of scale which make the holdings of a landowner a more efficient productive unit. This is not so. The owner of several rubber holdings does not integrate their operation into a single whole but rather has a separate bargain in relation to each holding with the share-tapper working it, and it might even be said that the owner is better regarded as a rentier rather than as an entrepreneur in his relation to the land and the share-tapper.

The most important way in which the character of Malay society affects the economy is in the field of values and attitudes. This cannot be treated as the impact of 'society' on 'the economy', for these attitudes colour the social system throughout, and cannot be identified with any specific area, as can the process of concentration of wealth with the economy. Value–attitudes such as fatalism, the short run orientation, the reluctance to alter an arrangement which is satisfactorily meeting minimum consumption needs, the contingent character of economic bargains, together with the factors which impede organization, such as the lack of legitimate leadership roles within the village, are of great importance in understanding the people's economic activity; above all its lack of dynamism, and weakness in the face of outside competition.

In my opinion value–attitude factors of this kind pose the major problems facing planners concerned with Malay economic development, rather than the specific issues such as lack of education or inadequacy of capital in which the causes of failure are usually found. The practical discussion of such issues is made difficult by the Malays' propensity to treat any comment as a slur on their racial character, and also by the lesser reality of cultural factors in the eyes of economic planners, as compared to, say, the objectivity of land acreages or investment values. It may be, however, that the strength of particularistic ties which have been such an important element in the Chinese economic system will not be so adaptable to the problems of universalistic efficiency which face the large bureaucratic concern; and that the Malay, who has made a successful bureacrat, may be able to play a larger part in the next stage of Malaya's economic development, typified by the growing number of large factories.

KINSHIP AND THE ECONOMY

I wish to discuss separately the part of kinship in general in economic life, and of matrilineal kinship in particular. Kinship in general refers to the distinction villagers make between people with whom they are connected, who are 'not strangers', and other people. Bilateral ties of consanguinity and affinal ties create bonds between individuals and should mean special favoured treatment for those with whom such ties exist. In theory the strength of the tie decreases with kinship distance, but as this is not a highly structured system there is considerable scope for variation with the personal relations of the actors.

In industrial society there is a radical divorce between kinship roles, now almost entirely confined to the domestic functions of the nuclear family, and occupational roles. In the Malay economy the household is the basic economic unit, and the concentration of both kinship ties and economic relations within a few villages means that the relationship between economy and kinship must be closer than in the industrial society.

A few generations ago kinship provided the framework for most social behaviour, and even today the emotional sanction behind kinship ties is still strong. Individuals fear the criticism that they are not treating their kin well, and feel obliged to give them special treatment. But what is striking in discussing these matters with the peasantry is the way in which they continually weigh their economic relations with kin against a purely economic relation with a non-relative, and express a clear preference for the latter. It is true that the individual feels a need for kin as a source of security in misfortune, and the only sure source of help in ceremonials or feasts. But such relationships are something one needs rather than things which are good or worthwhile in themselves. Obligation is what is stressed in contemporary kinship; the individual speaks as if he felt he were the loser from these reciprocal ties.

The trend of the social organization is in keeping with these attitudes. In religion the tendency is towards territorial bureaucratic organization and the abandonment of traditional kinship features. In rice cultivation large groups are less and less seen. A rich man building a house relies on hired labour, and at his child's wedding it is not unusual to find that the cooking is done on contract by a hired cook, and that the waiters at table are junior clerks and *peons* from his office, or members of the UMNO youth.

One clear effect of matrilineal kinship is to emphasize relations between *biras*, the husbands of sisters, for as a man's economic affairs centre on his family of procreation, dependence on kin, and obligations to kin, tend to mean particularly those kin occupying nearby houses.

Another consequence is seen in the ownership of property by women. This is more common throughout Malay society than the formal rules of Islamic law might suggest, but Negri Sembilan, where it is normal for women to own the ricefields and house sites, represents an extreme. Women inherit some property because the law requires that they receive it, but the system of inheritance is really controlled by law only in the event of disagreement. I have only been able to study inheritance through informants' reports, as there were no deaths of property owners in the village I was studying during my stay. These reports stress two elements, agreement and equality of shares between all siblings.

There are two legal systems which might apply to the inheritance of property. Where this property is registered as *pusaka* it will devolve according to *adat* rules if a case is taken to court. If it is not so registered the court will apply the shares specified in Islamic law. But according to village values a case should not reach court. It causes shame to quarrel over property at all between close kin, but especially so if outsiders must be brought in to settle the dispute. If one sibling is insistent on receiving a particular piece of property then he or she should receive it rather than quarrel. And shares should be equal for all siblings regardless of sex. The type of property siblings receive is affected by the economic roles of the sexes; rubber for men, and rice and homestead land for women, for these are the types of property they can use. But this allocation will be followed whatever the legal status of the land, and there is no rule which says that only men can inherit rubber. The shares should be regarded as equivalent in value, and this means that the daughter of wealthy parents will receive some rubber as part of her inheritance share.

Save for the issue of inheritance it is fair to say that the main specific consequence of matrilineal kinship for the economy is to determine which individuals will be most likely to have economic relations; it does little to differentiate the content of those relations from those with other kin.

The economy, emphasizing the importance of the household, makes for a further decline of corporate kinship groups, and the greater the dependance on rubber the greater this effect. Rubber tapping, and the need to purchase consumption goods, even limit the time which an individual is prepared to spend on ceremonial and other activities. Finally, the more a household depends on the productive activities of the husband, the less significant becomes whatever property the woman may have inherited from her *perut*.

My first hypothesis in undertaking field research in Jelebu was that the growth of a cash economy in Negri Sembilan would prove a major factor making for the decline of *adat perpateh*, and a major source of strain between upholders of clan rights in land and others preferring individual disposal. Had my expectations been fulfilled there would have been an even closer connection between my two areas of special attention, matrilineal kinship and the peasant economy, than in fact emerged. This I attribute to underestimating the significance of modern political and administrative change. The effects which I had expected to follow from the introduction of rubber may be seen, but they reacted on a matrilineal system which was already greatly weakened. For example, even if the creation of rubber holdings did increase the desire for individual ownership of land by males the land on which the holdings were planted had been removed from *adat* control in 1891, more than 20 years before the villagers began rubber planting. Similarly, although a man may be more independent of the control of both his own kin and the *tempat semanda* when he derives his income from a rubber holding, this is a further factor weakening an already weak kin control.

The evidence from other parts of Negri Sembilan supports the view that there was a clash between two opinions on the control of property occasioned by the importance of new forms of landed wealth, and that this clash was a factor undermining *adat*. It is possible that I arrived in Jelebu too late to observe this process, but it is unlikely that a process still continuing in Rembau (De Jong, 1960) would have been completed in Jelebu. My hypothesis would rather be that land shortage is a necessary condition for quarrelling within the kin group about land, with different parties stressing *adat*/female and *shariat*/male claims, and that land shortage is more serious in Rembau than Jelebu. (Agoes Salim, 1958.)

The absence of complex organizational problems in the Malay village economy limits the value of this study as a contribution to the discussion of peasant economic systems. Many of the more interesting questions about an economy do not arise when economic activity is confined to small-scale production of agricultural goods, with processing and sale in the hands of other ethnic groups; especially so as the economy at the time of study was in a routine phase when most producers were confronted with only minor decisions concerning the use of assets already in existence in fixed form.

Two purely economic processes of change were to be observed.

Firstly the trend towards concentration of property, and secondly the trend towards exclusive dependence on rubber production to meet all consumption needs. Both processes represent the working out of change begun with the adoption of rubber growing by the peasantry in 1916.

Since this study was completed the Government has undertaken an extensive programme of rural development, and further field research is sure to be rewarding as the observer will be able to study the effects of this programme and the reactions of the peasantry, instead of the fairly prosperous but static conditions which obtained during my stay.

Glossary

abang: elder brother.

adat perpateh: the matrilineal custom, named after the culture hero Dato Perpateh nan Sabatang.

adek: younger sibling.

alim: learned, pious.

amil: official collector of *fitrah*.

anak: child.

anakbuah: kin, especially of a chief.

ayer: water.

ayerkaki: literally 'water of the feet', this expression is an abbreviation of the phrase *ayer akan membasoh kaki tangan*, water to wash the feet and hands, used of the clan in a special relationship to a raja, e.g. the Batu Hampar of Sri Menanti.

balai: any public building, but in Negri Sembilan particularly where the Undang holds audience.

bangsat: impoverished – derogatory term.

baroh: the land below.

berkampong: to foregather.

bersanding: the sitting in state of bride and groom which forms a major part of a Malay wedding ceremonial.

biasa: accustomed.

biduanda: the superior (original?) clans.

bilal: caller to prayer in a mosque.

biras: wife's sister's husband.

bujang: single person of marriageable age.

charian: thing found or acquired, from *chari* to seek.

dapatan: thing obtained, from *dapat* to obtain.

darat: the land above.

dukun: magician specializing in cures and other private magic.

dusun: orchard.

fitrah: an obligatory payment of one Bagdadi bushel of the staple grain, or its cash equivalent, at the end of the fasting month.

ganti: replacement, to replace.

getah: rubber.

gila: mad.

haj: the pilgrimage to Mecca, one of the Five Pillars of Islam.

haji: someone who has made the pilgrimage to Mecca, an honorific.

hari raya: feast days to celebrate the end of the fasting month (*hari raya puasa*) and the day of sacrifice during the Meccan pilgrimage.

harta: property.

hasil tanah: land rent or product, the payments made to Biduanda in commutation of their former land rights.

hewan: beast.

hutang: obligation, debt.

ibubapa: sub-clan chief.

imam: prayer leader.

janda: widow or divorcee.

kadi: Muslim judge.

kadim: relationship, used of ceremonially created matrilineal connection; to create such connection.

kahwin: marry.

kakak: older sister.

kampong: village, homestead.

kati: weight measure of $1\frac{1}{3}$ pounds (English form, *katty*).

Kaum Ibu: lit. womenfolk, the woman's section of the United

Malay Nationalist Organization (U M N O).

keramat: miracle-working persons, things or places.

ketua: leader.

kutu: type of loan association.

lebai: honorific for religious specialist, generally one who has not yet made the pilgrimage and so cannot be addressed as *Tuan Haji.*

lembaga: clan chief.

luak: *adat* district.

malu: shame (a very broad and very important concept).

mati: to die, dead.

Maulud Nabi: the birthday of the Prophet and its celebration.

menantu: child-in-law.

mentua: parent-in-law.

menyembah: make obeisance.

menyeraya: ceremonially organized cooperative work.

muafakat: agreement (more usually pronouned *pakat*).

mukim: area surrounding a mosque from which the minimum congregation of 40 is drawn, but nowadays, a division of an administrative district.

niat: wish, desire; vow made to a *keramat.*

orang semanda: man in role of affine towards wife's kin.

pahala: religious reward.

pajak: to buy fruit on the tree for a lump sum; to rent a rubber holding for a fixed sum regardless of yield; to mortgage a fruit holding until a loan is repaid.

paksa: to force; compulsory.

pawang: magician especially concerned with social rites.

penghulu: official in charge of a *mukim,* in *adat* applied to the *Undang.*

perbilangan: traditional saying.

perut: stomach, womb, sub-clan.

pikul: weight of 133 lbs. or 100 *kati.*

pulut: glutinous rice.

pusaka: inheritance, inherited.

raja: prince, ruler.

rayat: subject, but used in Jelebu of aborigines.

rembas: the light, sharp Malay hoe.

rezeki: one's economic fate.

Syed: title of reputed descendants of the Prophet.

suku: quarter, clan.

tabal: the installation of an *Undang.*

taboh melukut: scatter rice-siftings, as if feeding chickens.

tahan: to restrain.

talak: the divorce formula.

tanah pusaka: ancestral land.

tempat semanda: the wife's kin seen as a collectivity.

tengku: prince.

tiga: three; *tiga suku:* threequarters and hence, 'not all there'.

timbang salah: literally 'to weigh the wrong', the feast given by wrong-doers.

tolong: to help; *tolong-menolong:* informal work cooperation.

tumpang: joining in with others.

ugama: religion.

ulama: religious scholar.

Undang: *adat* chief, ruler of a *luak.*

wakaf: property dedicated to religious purposes.

wali: guardian.

waris: heirs, in Negri Sembilan applied to the clan.

Yang-di-Pertuan Besar (abbrev. *Yam-Tuan*): ruler of the state.

zakat: annual religious tithe.

Bibliography

The following abbreviated references are used: The Journal of the Straits Branch of the Royal Asiatic Society, *JSBRAS*; the Journal of the Malayan Branch, *JMBRAS*; the series Papers on Malay Subjects, *PMS*.

AHMAD DT. BATUAH and A. DT. MADJOINDO, 1956. *Tambo Minangkabau*, Djakarta.

AZIZ BIN KHAMIS, A., 1936. 'Adat Kuala Pilah', *JMBRAS*, XIV, 3.

BAUER, P. T., 1946. 'The Working of Rubber Regulation', *Economic Journal*, LVI. (Reprinted in T. H. Silcock, 1961.)

—— 1957. 'Malayan Rubber Policy', *Political Science Quarterly*, LXXII, 1. (Reprinted in T. H. Silcock, 1961.)

BURRIDGE, K. O. L., 1957. 'Rural Administration in Johore', *Journal of African Administration*, 9, 1.

CALDECOTT, A., 1912. *Jelebu: Its History and Constitution*, PMS.

—— 1917. 'Jelebu Customary Songs and Sayings', *JSBRAS*, LXXVIII.

DJAMOUR, J., 1952. 'Adoption of Children among Singapore Malaysians', *Journal of the Royal Anthropological Institute*, LXXXII, 2.

—— 1959. *Malay Kinship and Marriage in Singapore*, London.

EGGAN, F., 1949. 'The Hopi and the Lineage Principle', in *Social Structure*, ed. Fortes, M., London.

FIRTH, RAYMOND, 1939. *Primitive Polynesian Economy*, London.

—— 1946. *Malay Fishermen: Their Peasant Economy*, London.

—— 1951. *Elements of Social Organization*, London.

FIRTH, ROSEMARY, 1943. *Housekeeping among Malay Peasants*, London.

GULLICK, J. M., 1946. 'The Election of an Undang of Jelebu', *Man*, XLVI, 104.

—— 1949. 'Sungai Ujong', *JMBRAS*, XXII, 2.

—— 1951. 'The Negri Sembilan Economy of the 1890's', *JMBRAS*, XXII, 38.

—— 1958. *Indigenous Political Systems of Western Malaya*, London.

INTERNATIONAL BANK FOR RECONSTRUCTION AND DEVELOPMENT, 1955. *The Economic Development of Malaya*, Baltimore.

DE JOSSELIN DE JONG, P. E., 1951. *Minangkabau and Negri Sembilan*, Leiden.

—— 1956. 'De Visie der Participanten op hun Cultuur', *Bijdragen tot de Taal-, Land- en Volkenkunde*, 112, 2.

—— 1960. 'Islam versus Adat in Negri Sembilan (Malaya)', *Bijdragen tot de Taal-, Land- en Volkenkunde*, 116, 1.

KAHAR BIN BADOR, A., 1960. *Adat Perpatih di Tanah Mengandong*. (MS deposited with the Department of Malay Studies, University of Malaya.)

MYRDAL, G., 1957. *Economic Theory and the Underdeveloped Regions*, London.

PARR, C. W. C. and MACKRAY, W. H., 1910., Rembau: One of the Nine States', *JSBRAS*, 56.

PARSONS, T., *Structure and Process in Modern Societies*, Glencoe, 1960.

RICHARDS, A. I., 1950. 'Some Types of Family Structure amongst the Central Bantu', in *African Systems of Kinship and Marriage*, eds. Radcliffe-Brown, A. R. and Forde, D. C., London.

SALIM, A., 1958. *The Impact of Adat Perpateh on Land Ownership*. (MS deposited with the Department of Economics, University of Singapore.)

SCHRIEKE, B., 1955. *Indonesian Sociological Studies*, I, The Hague.

SILCOCK, T. H., 1961. *Readings in Malayan Economics*, Singapore.

SITUMORANG, T. D. and TEEUW, A. (eds.), 1952. *Sedjarah Melaju*, Djakarta.

SWIFT, M. G., 1957. 'The Accumulation of Capital in a Peasant Economy', *Economic Development and Cultural Change*, V, 4. (Reprinted in T. H. Silcock, 1961.)

— — 1958. 'A Note on the Durability of Malay Marriages', *Man*, LVIII, 208.

— — 1962. 'Malay Peasants', in *The Role of Savings and Wealth in Southern Asia and the West*, eds. Lambert, R. D. and Hoselitz, B.

— — 1963. 'Capital, Saving and Credit in Malay Peasant Economy', in *Capital, Saving and Credit in Peasant Societies*, eds. Firth, R. and Yamey, B. S., London.

SYED HUSSIN ALI, 1960. *Susunlapis Masharakat di-Kampong Bagan: Batu Pahat*. (MS. A revised and expanded English version of this work was accepted for the degree of M.A. in the Department of Malay Studies, University of Malaya.)

WERTHEIM, W. F., 1959. *Indonesian Society in Transition*, The Hague.

WILKINSON, R. J., 1912. *Sri Menanti*, *PMS*, Kuala Lumpur.

Index

LONDON SCHOOL OF ECONOMICS
MONOGRAPHS ON SOCIAL ANTHROPOLOGY

Titles marked with an asterisk are now out of print. Those marked with a dagger have been reprinted in paperback editions and are only available in this form.

747 / 70